For Sorcha,
Every be
Marg

Angel Love – a Workbook

by

Margaret Neylon

Angels Bring Love, Warwick, England.

First published 1996.
Revised and updated 2004.

Angel Love – A Workbook, 2004
published by Angels Bring Love, Warwick, England.
01962 316307 www.angelsbringlove.com

British Library Cataloguing in Publication Data
Neylon, Margaret
Angel Love –A Workbook

ISBN: 0-9547958-0-6

Cover Design: John Willcott, Charlie Flounders and Steven Harris
Typesetting, Origination and Printing: PCS Typesetting and CPI Bath
Cover Illustration: Theresa Erasmus

Contents

Dedication

To those who have supported me,
a million thanks!

Introduction

I shall always remember June 29th 1994. It was a beautifully sunny day and I was lying out in my garden in Dublin, lazily looking up at the clear blue sky, when a voice said distinctly in my left ear 'Give a course called Talking With Angels'. I recognised the voice because I've heard it so often over the years. It's the voice of my angel.

I wrote down the message immediately. Being clairaudient (someone who hears beyond the norm) I know it's essential not to leave messages to memory alone so I write down the

words precisely as I hear them. At that moment I knew I would give a course called 'Talking With Angels' as requested, but I hadn't a clue as to how to go about such an enterprise. Back then, a decade ago, very few people talked about angels and there was little reference material. However, I took the plunge and advertised my course, committing myself to a date ten weeks ahead. I still didn't know how to lead such a course, but I knew I'd find the answers, all I had to do was ask for help from my angels. So I did, and they replied in many ways: I was prompted to pick up specific books and magazines at random in which I found many unexpected references to angels; my ears tuned into the myriad of songs coming over the air waves in which our celestial friends are mentioned, and during my sleeping hours I was given a lot of guidance.

Soon people began to make enquiries about this unique course and I began to realise just how timely the message had been. Strangers were saying 'It's such a relief to talk to someone about my angel' and 'You've heard them too!' The response was amazing. It began as a trickle of interested individuals and now, ten years later, I regularly give workshops all over Ireland, the

UK, Europe, South Africa and even Australia! I've guested on many radio and tv shows, been interviewed by newspaper and magazine journalists, and even been featured on Sky TV News! Where I had once feared scepticism, I've been delighted to see in people's eyes a growing recognition and understanding as they have been gently reminded of their wonderful, everlasting friends.

Since bringing out my first book on angels 'Open Your Heart to Angel Love' in 1996, I've also had 'Angel Magic' and 'An Angel a Day' published (by Thorsons/Element) and my life has been transformed in many different ways. I know that if you, too, open to Angel Love your life can also change for the better. Remember you can enjoy your angel's love at all times, but you must remember to ask for help and be willing to make the changes necessary to bring about that needed transformation. As human beings we tend to close ourselves up out of fear, instead of opening our hearts to their love.

Try not to jam all the exercises within this book into a couple of days. Take time to get to know yourself and your angel a little more. And most of all, have fun!

As I always say: 'You're never alone, you've an angel'. And now you're on your way to opening up your heart to yours.

Margaret Neylon, 2004

You're Never Alone

You're never alone, you've an angel
Although it may seem far away
Somewhere up in the sky, above where the clouds fly
But that's where they come from, not where they reside
You just have to call them to be by your side
'Cos you're never alone, you've an angel.

You're never alone, you've an angel
(At least one, if not two or more)
You ask them a question, await the reply
Through tv, the post, or in bed while you lie
Asleep, deep in dreaming, and when you awake
Your reasoning, trance-like, your head needs a shake.
Make the first thing you do upon waking each day
To record your dream travels and see what they say
They may be a message sent down from above
To help you, to guide you, to fill you with love.
'Cos you're never alone, you've an angel.

So if you feel lonely, or if you feel blue
There's an angel beside you to help you, it's true
'Cos you're never alone, you've an angel
Now open your heart up, it's waiting for you.

By Margaret Neylon, 1994.

Step 1:
Opening Up to Your Angel

'We are born to walk with angels
But instead, we search for jewels in the mud.'

Angel love is different from any other love we can ever hope to receive. It is given to us totally and absolutely without any conditions attached. We do not have to be perfect, we do not have to be smart, we do not have to attain any great success in our lives in order to receive it. It does not matter how apparently 'undeserving' we feel we may be. Angel love is there for us. All we need do is be open to it. Then we can see 'with angel eyes' and offer others the

unconditional love we have enjoyed. And when we are filled with this angelic love our lives change, perhaps in simple ways, perhaps in miraculous ways.

So why are many people unaware that this love is there for them? Quite simply, because some are not open to it. Often I visualise angels sitting about in our homes and work-places patiently knitting away. Angels need all the patience in the world (and beyond it) because so few of us ever listen. They're here to guide us and help us along our life path yet we humans tend to be so contrary, refusing to get their angelic messages. It's a wonder they haven't left us centuries ago! Fortunately angels have a sense of humour and an oceanful of forgiveness for us mortals, which is why they're still here.

I know in my own case I must have been a great trial to my angels because, although I've always known they were about, I did ignore them for many years. You see, until my twenties I thought everyone knew they had an angel who gave them messages, so I didn't ever think to bring it up in conversation. To me it was a fact of life, just as the Earth is round, or the Moon shines at night, or that rain is needed to make things grow. Then, when

I was in my 20s, I mentioned some message I'd received to my boyfriend at the time. His reaction was less than supportive. In fact he laughed and teased me about it, and I ended up feeling that I was the odd one out, that I must be crazy to think I was hearing messages from, of all things, an angel! Being a very dependent person at that time I chose to believe him instead of my inner self, and turned a deaf ear to my best friend of all time, my angel. Fortunately I've since become involved in the healing field and since I began to open up to my psychic abilities I now to hear my angels and often see them too.

The best way to write this book is to share with you some of my own experiences and in this first chapter answer the many questions which are put to me at workshops and by the media. I have no doubt that if you participate in the exercises as set out here – the relaxation exercises and the workpages, you will encounter your own angel (or angels) and open up your heart to angel love.

Aren't angels just for kids? That's a question I'm often asked over the airwaves. No, they're for everyone, no matter what age, race or creed. In fact, all the major religions of the world recog-

nise their existence. They've been manifesting for people, regardless of their faith, for centuries. In the Old Testament of the Bible alone angels crop up regularly: when Abraham was about to sacrifice his son Isaac, an angel stayed his hand; Daniel was saved from death in the lion's den by an angel, and there's a lovely story about Tobias and his angel who joined him on a long and arduous journey. In the New Testament Mary was told by Angel Gabriel that she was to bear Jesus, and an angel later came to Joseph to warn him that Herod's soldiers were looking for the young infant. There are many references again to angels in the New Testament, especially in the Book of Revelations. The Islamic faith tells us that the Angel Gabriel dictated the Koran to the Prophet Mohammed who was later transported to Paradise by a host of angels. Across the Atlantic Ocean in the mid-1800s a man named Joseph Smith was given specific information by the Angel Moroni which resulted in the formation of the Mormon Church. Despite the many references to angels in these holy books, adults in particular still tend to treat angels as though they were from a child's fairy tale. Perhaps it's because we've become used to only believing in 'empirically proven'

things. So, if our scientists cannot poke and prod at an angelic being and put a sample under a microscope, they tend to dismiss them.

Yet children have no problem believing in angels. Perhaps it's because they're often able to see them! (They haven't started learning science subjects yet.) During my early school years we were taught about 'Guardian Angels' and we used to say a short prayer: 'Oh Angel of God, my guardian dear, to whom God's love commits me here, ever this day be at my side, to light and guard, to rule and guide'.

Then, somehow, around the time when we tend to lose sight of Father Christmas, we seem to lose our memory of our angels. However, though I left my angels they did not leave me. What happens to us that, as children, we can understand, accept and communicate with these celestial beings, yet when we apparently become 'mature' we refuse to acknowledge them?

Fear of ridicule kept me away from mine, and maybe it is just a simple problem of peer pressure and teasing that shuts down our senses to them. What a shame, because I know how lonely some people can feel, how frightened they can be of being

alone. These people need to know they can't be alone because they do have an angel, whether they like it or not! Angels are with us, with each of us, whether we accept them or reject them. They do, however, need to work on a 'need to know' basis, only butting in unasked when we've been threatened in some way. So if we want to hear from them for whatever reason we must ask for help. Then, in return, we will be given an answer in one of several ways: by a 'co-incidence', by a friend, by a voice within or a thought, by a stranger of by 'an angel in disguise'. Take a moment or two now to recall all those 'inspired' guesses, those 'fortuitous' phone calls, those 'chance' meetings which have patchworked your life. And how often has someone 'appeared out of the blue' to help when you've really needed it? Was it a co-incidence, or was it the angels synchronising these events?

So what are angels all about? The word 'angel' comes from the Greek 'angelos' which means 'God's messenger'. So angels are messengers from God. I believe we are each brought to Earth to learn certain lessons, become enlightened with that knowledge and move back to the brilliance of the ultimate

power which, depending on your religious beliefs, we call God, Creation, or the Light Force.

As we're here to learn certain lessons you might think of life along the lines of being back at school. We're all at the Earth School, and that means no-one is either superior or inferior to me or anyone else: we are all equal because we are all students. Not one of us is perfect: we are not meant to be, that is why we are here. When I state this in my workshops most people breathe a great sigh. What a relief, we now have no need to pretend to be perfect! We can each be ourselves at last. However, some of us are in different 'grades' and it is up to those in higher grades to aid those coming behind.

When we learn one lesson we go on to the next and often people we taught about one subject can now become our teachers for a different subject that we need to learn. It's a bit like a bicycle wheel: I see the outer rim, the tyre, as being the route we travel along in our life. The angels are the 'middle men', being half way between the spokes and the wheel's centre, the hub, which is God. Each of us begins and ends at a different point along this tyre, but we each are the same distance from

God. During our life's journey we can ask for help from other people, from our higher self and, of course, from our angels. Our angels, those 'messengers from God', are always there for us, we just have to remember to ask for help when we need it.

Often I'm asked the difference between angels and spiritual guides. Are they the same, or different? Angels are beings of light which come directly from God. I do not believe that angels have ever lived as human beings (except on occasion when they take human form for short periods) because they are beings of perfection, coming directly from God and, unlike us, they do not need to learn any lessons. On the other hand, Spiritual Guides were once human beings who have, for some reason, agreed to remain with us in spirit in order to guide us along in our life. No doubt our own spirit could make a similar agreement to do the same for someone else if need be.

Both can be called 'spiritual guides', however, because they do bring guidance on the spiritual level. Please don't waste energy wondering where good advice comes from when you're in a time of need. Just listen to it and act on it! The more you connect with your spiritual self, the easier it will become to differentiate between them. There is more on this subject later in this book on the section regarding dreams.

So can we learn anything from angels? We certainly can. Angels offer us loving understanding and unconditional love. They come to us here on Earth in order to help us increase our ability for loving understanding and unconditional love for others. By doing so they connect with us at the highest level at which we are capable of functioning, and when this is achieved we extend and expand our capacity for growth and transformation. In this way we become enlightened and fulfil our life's purpose on this Earth.

As I stated earlier, I believe we've all come here in order to learn certain lessons. In this school called Planet Earth we find that some lessons are easy, and some are hard. Look back to the time when you were are in elementary or secondary school. When you were at your lessons and you made a mistake, what did you do? Most likely you did the exercise again and, if you learned from your mistake you got it right this time and then went onto the next lesson. However, we're so hard on ourselves when we become adults! If we do something wrong now, if we make a mistake, we often never forgive our-

selves. Can you imagine how unbelievable it would be if a teacher refused to forgive a pupil for making a mistake at school? Every parent would be outraged at such treatment! We really must learn to forgive ourselves for all our mistakes, little or large. After all, we're here to learn, and if we knew everything we would not be here in the first place! So we must learn to have unconditional love for ourselves, just as our angels do. Then, when the dull negativity that weighs us down so much has gone from our lives we shall be able to walk with our angels, instead of searching for jewels in the mud.

Why do some people have a problem believing angels really exist? I feel it is because nowadays we live in a society which has based most of its judgements on empirical science, which states that something has to be proven by scientific research before it can be believed. No doubt it was the mushrooming of empirical science in the last two hundred years or so that led us to lose sight of our angelic friends. We don't usually see or touch our angels so therefore scientists say they cannot exist. Can that be so? Do we really need to see or touch something in order to know it exists?

Think for a moment about what happens if you turn on a

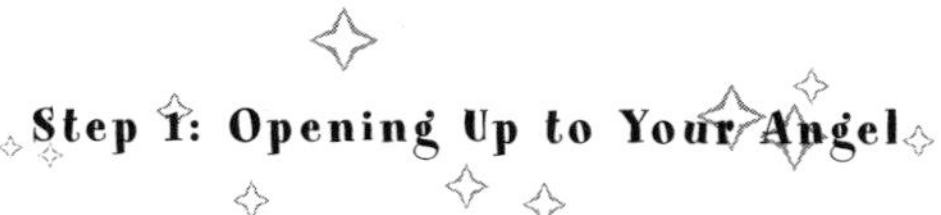

radio. A voice or a sound comes out of it. But you cannot touch this voice or sound, and you cannot see it either. So does this mean it doesn't exist? Are you crazy if you hear it? Of course not! The voice or sound most definitely exists, but it's being transmitted through a different vibration or energy, through sound waves. Angels operate on a different vibration too, they operate on the light vibration. That's why it's not always so easy for them to manifest into a form we can see with our eyes. But they can do it, if it is really necessary.

It is possible for each of us to see our angels, but we do tend to see them in our own unique way. Angels are individual to each of us. Because they are truly Beings of Light they don't have a body. They are neither male nor female as they do not need to physically reproduce themselves, but often the angel that comes to you may 'seem' female or male, depending on the kind of help you need at the time. Despite the fact that they are beings of light energy and have no density or material substance, angels can and often do show themselves in one way or another .

My own angels manifest for me as small golden orbs of light

which show themselves on the walls first, thus catching my eye, then dance around the room. These orbs of light are brilliant gold in colour with an ever-pulsing centre of red-gold energy. They first appeared for me when I was going through a very depressed state, when my career seemed to have crashed around me and I was living in great fear of poverty and isolation. They used to come regularly when I first began my workshops, as though they were saying 'See, we're here for you!' but now they don't show themselves quite so often. I sometimes wish I could see them all the time, but I know this isn't the point, so now I accept it that way. In my workshops I often see at least one angel manifest within the room, especially when the group's energy is flowing and heightened. At such times it's like seeing the outline of a human form in pure golden light with seemingly an addition of pure light behind it. This golden light is like no other light I've ever seen. It's as though it's made of gold yet it has a vibrancy and brightness behind it that is definitely out of this world! The Light Beings also move very quickly from one spot to another. It's as if they're saying 'No, you're not imagining this. I am here, watch me move around!'

They are not auras of the people in the group, because auras are different. I've never felt frightened when I see these beings. On the contrary I feel filled with joy, because I know they are telling me I have finally found my pathway in life and I need have no fear of my present or future any more because they are always here, looking after me. Some people taking part in the workshops have also seen an angel as though it was standing close behind me.

At first it seemed to me as though angels have wings, but in fact it is simply the impression we get of the golden light radiating outwards and upwards from the Light Being's centre. I believe that the reason we humans have painted angels with wings over the centuries is because we knew they were from 'above', i.e. the lighter vibration, and the only way we could imagine them travelling was to give them wings just like the birds who fly above too. I might add that angels will manifest themselves for us in a way that is acceptable and non-threatening. Therefore, if you can only imagine an angel having wings and you want to see one, that is most likely the form it will take for you. If you prefer to imagine your angel with long golden

hair carrying a lute, or perhaps as a friendly old man, then these are the ways you will see your angel. When it comes to your angel, anything is possible! Without knowing it, you may already have been given an inkling that your angel is about you. Because angels come to us from the light vibration they travel at the speed of light, which is very fast indeed, almost too fast for us to follow. Often people see flashes of bright light seemingly just out of the corner of their eye, or perhaps on a wall, or close to someone else. Have you ever seen a bright flash of light move very quickly across your vision or seen small bright lights moving around your home? If you've ever thought 'I must be seeing things!' you were quite right, the 'things' you were seeing were angels!

As I mentioned in the Introduction, I am clairaudient, which means I hear messages, and am also developing my clairvoyance, which is to see beyond the norm. You may be neither of these, but you may sense things. This is to be 'clairsentient', to have clear senses. Another way an angel will tell you it's close by is by offering you a strong scent of perfume, just as though a bouquet of flowers is in front of you in reality. I remember driving quite a long distance after giving a weekend workshop down the country and feeling quite exhausted. Suddenly, it was as though the whole car was filled with a fresh scent of pine. The vibrancy of the pine essence enlivened me again. I had a friend with me in the car at the time and she also smelt it. So do be aware of the many ways your angel can let you know it's around.

Often people 'see' their angel in their mind's eye only, or they may feel with an absolute certainty a warmth beside them or a glow of love surrounding them. Or perhaps their angels might prove their closeness by sending them a wonderful musical score in their mind, or a burst of vibrant, heavenly colour. We can each connect with our angel in our own unique way and any way is the right way for you. When I am giving a Guided Meditation during my workshops sometimes a participant feels a hand holding theirs and is convinced it is mine, or they may feel as though I am shining a bright light into their closed eyes. These are all messages from angels who are just trying to say 'Hi, I'm close by!'

Sometimes, in times of great need, angels can appear as just ordinary people: ordinary people who show us an extraordinary kindness or bring an extraordinary sense of peace along with them, or perhaps pass on some precise knowledge which is essential to us at that moment. The important thing is not to ignore it, or to dis-believe its help due to a mind-set of negative thought patterns within oneself.

So why doesn't everyone see angels all the time if they are around us? I think it's because we have been taught to be fearful of things we do not understand. Fear is the greatest destroyer of love and trust. If we could cancel fear completely from our lives we would all be communicating with our angels, whether we can see them or not. Of course, fear can be okay in the correct context: when there is a large articulated truck bearing down on you it's good to feel enough fear to get out of the way, or if you smell smoke in the middle of the night it's good to feel enough fear to propel you out of the house. But when fear is inappropriate to the situation – such as being fearful because we are lacking in knowledge – it can be self-destructive. Can you imagine a world full of people who look on each other with love instead of fear? It is possible to change from fear to love, once we open our heart to our angel.

The reason I have written this book is to help you overcome any fear you may be holding onto which is stopping you opening up your heart to the greatest, most loving friend of all: your angel.

The main benefits of connecting with our angelic friends can be felt in many ways in our lives. If you are working on your own, without any angelic help, you can draw only on what you feel, what you think, and what you know. So that means you're probably struggling through life right now, and you're most certainly living in limitation in some way. Ask your angel to be with you and you can enjoy mutual collaboration without any limits because you will then be plugged into a vast store of knowledge from the Universal Mind which is just waiting to be tapped. It is a bit like having a computer and switching into the Internet. Immediately you can tap into a huge source of knowledge and guidance. By co-operating with your celestial friends you can enjoy a little piece of heaven. The word 'heaven' means 'harmony' and the word 'hell' means 'wall' or 'boundary'. Working alone, by putting a wall or boundary around us, we are living in isolation and loneliness, and this does feel like a 'living

hell'. With our angel beside us, however, we know we are no longer alone, and can always call out for help and guidance, no matter the problem.

What do angels expect in return? The answer to that question is very little, except that we try to be open to the truth, that we try to speak the truth, and that we show enthusiasm and gratitude for their presence. By showing something as simple as gratitude it is possible to receive miracles in return. Angels want to be with us, they want to connect with us, and they want to share with us their light, their levity and their love.

Angel Message Cards

Did you know that we are spirits who happen to have bodies, rather than bodies which happen to have spirits? Are you aware that our conscious, awake self is only about 10% of our entire being? The other 90% is our spiritual or unconscious part, also known as the Higher Self. Often our conscious self is called our 'Ego' and it is our ego which gets us up in the morning, propels us out the door to work or whatever is required for the day, makes our decisions, forms judgements, and all the while the remaining 90% of our being is keeping quiet while our ego takes charge. That 90% – the Higher Self – is the part of us that is connected with Creation and with God. It is that part of us that connects with our angels, where everything is possible if we just remember to ask for guidance.

There is now a wide selection of angel message cards available on the market. During my workshops I use 'Angel Cards' to bring instant and loving messages into people's lives. These 'Angel Cards' are a pack of 52 finger-length cards created at the Findhorn Foundation in Scotland in order to develop inner consciousness and help the user focus on particular aspects of their life at the time. They are available in many outlets nowadays. On each card is an appropriate picture of an angel along with a keyword such as 'Love', 'Forgiveness', 'Trust', 'Compassion', 'Healing', etc.

This is a very simple way to get in touch with your angel and help overcome any fear regarding such a connection. I begin my workshops by setting out those Angel Cards face down and asking each participant to pick one. The card they choose is the gift they receive from their angel for that week, and it's quite

astonishing how pertinent the messages prove to be!

Over the years I have received many clairaudient messages to help me along my path, and I have recorded them. When I was developing my Talking With Angels workshop I was inspired to include these messages in the course. I call them 'Angel Inspiration Cards' and they have now been developed into a boxed set of 50 different messages, most of which I have received myself, and others which come from other sources such as The Bible. The Angel Inspiration Cards are also used for guidance and support as we move through the workshop and our life's path.

Opening up to your angel's love can be a lot of fun. Although it's not unusual to be afraid of something we do not see, try not to be fearful of your angels. Welcome them into your life. They've known you inside and out from the very first instant you came into existence. They know your good bits and your bad bits. And they still love you.

How to Use This Book

In each chapter you will find one or two special exercises which will help you open your heart to angel love. Most of these are based on visualisation or relaxation exercises, and you will need to be guided in these by a pre-recorded voice. Unless you are being led by a workshop facilitator it's best to record this in your own voice if possible, or in that of a trusted friend. Each of these exercises should take about 20 minutes, so make sure that the words are spoken slowly, leaving lots of long pauses during the instructions so that when you undergo the exercise you will have time to be able to really enjoy it. If you like you can play some soothing, gentle music quietly in the background. Make certain that the volume is low so that your spirit can drift off on its journey when you play it. (If you'd prefer to buy these pre-recorded, there is information at the back of this book on availability of my CD's or audio cassettes).

As you will see as you go through Angel Love, there are special 'Workpages' devoted to you to keep notes on your experiences as you go through this book. Keep a pen handy so that you can immediately record what happened on returning after the meditation. Everything you see, especially any colours, will be of importance.

Often when you are leading a busy life it can at first appear difficult to still your mind. The moment you try to relax your mind begins to filter in thoughts such as 'Did I lock the back door?' 'I wish that dog would stop barking!' 'What shall I prepare for supper?' and all sorts of niggling queries. Try not to fight these thoughts, that only connects you with your mind rather than your spirit. Instead, let the thoughts float in, and they will soon float out again if they are ignored. Then, before you know it, your spirit will be to the forefront and you will be enjoying your visualisation. Should you have any moment of fear as you let your mind drift, just say a word such as 'Love' or 'Angel' or 'Safe' and you will find this comes in and send any fear on its way.

If you are recording these in your own voice, you may prefer to change the word 'you' into the personal pronoun 'I', so record it the way you prefer.

Exercise 1: Earth Connection

Before doing any meditation or visualisation, it's always necessary to first ground yourself. This is a simple exercise. All you need do is follow these steps:

Make sure nothing will disturb you, so unhook the phone or turn on the answering machine, turn off your mobile, put the cat out, and stick up a 'Do Not Disturb' sign on your closed door if necessary! The next requirement is that you begin to relax. If you have not enjoyed relaxation exercises before, know that this is a simple exercise of just quietening the mind in order to get in touch with your spiritual self, otherwise known as your Higher Self. Relaxation is also very good for your physical health. You can often feel as though you've had a good night's sleep after a simple 10 or 15 minute relaxation exercise.

The most important thing to do now is to find a comfortable place for you to sit. (It's better to sit up, as if you lie down you may go to sleep!) Then close your eyes and begin to breathe in deeply and slowly. As you breathe in count to three, hold it for three seconds, then breathe out and imagine little roots are growing out from the soles of your feet into the ground. See

them being any colour you wish, and any size you wish, just so long as you find it relaxing and easy to do.

Now repeat the inhaling and exhaling for a few minutes, and each time you should feel these roots are firmly growing into the ground or floor beneath your feet.

You can vary this 'grounding' or 'earth connection' exercise if you wish, by simply changing the imagined roots into magnets. Visualise magnets developing on the soles of your feet and know that your feet are kept firmly on the ground due to the magnetism of the Earth below.

Exercise 2: Harmonising Your Energy

Now that you are grounded you are ready to enjoy a Guided Visualisation. The following is a suggested script:

When you're in a comfortable position, take a deep breath and as you breathe in imagine there's a beautiful blue light travelling up your toes, across your feet and into your ankles, and as you breathe out allow any tension in this area to gently flow out into the ground below.

Now as you breathe in, the beautiful blue light travels up from your ankles into your calves, and moves up into your knees. And as you breathe out allow any tension in this area to gently flow out into the ground below.

And as you breathe in, the beautiful blue light travels up from your knees into your thighs, and up into your hips. And as you breathe out allow any tension in this area to gently flow out into the ground below.

As you breathe in, the beautiful blue light travels around your hips and into your pelvis. The blue light travels all around your lower torso and into the base of your spine. And as you breathe out allow any tension in this area to gently flow out into the ground below.

Now breathe in the blue light into your upper torso. See the blue light travel into your heart and into your lungs. Now it moves up into your shoulders. And as you breathe out allow any tension in this area to gently flow out into the ground below.

Now as you breathe in, the beautiful blue light travels all around your shoulders, releasing any knots and tension there.

It flows gently down into your upper arms, your lower arms, and into your finger tips. And as you breathe out any tension in this area gently flows down into the ground below.

Now breathe in the beautiful blue light up into your throat and into your neck. The blue light releases any blocks in your throat and you find it easier to express yourself creatively. And now the blue light moves up into the back of your head, And as you breathe out any tension in this area gently flows out into the ground below.

Watch as the blue light moves up into your ears, helping to heal your hearing. Now it moves into your chin and your mouth, into your nose, up into your eyes and your forehead and now it goes all the way to the crown of your head. And as you breathe out any tension in this area gently flows into the ground below. And you know that the Earth will recycle anything you have given it and turn it into light.

You know now that you are filled from the tips of your toes to the top of your head with blue healing light. And as you gently breathe in and out you feel healing take place all over your body, and in particular in any place where there is a blockage of energy. Take a few moments to enjoy this wonderful feeling. How beautiful it is to be filled with healing blue light. How happy and content you feel!

Now I want you to imagine that you're in your favourite country place. Look around you. What a beautiful sight it is. And how quiet! All you can hear is bird song and the sound of my voice. You feel completely relaxed and at peace as you look around you. And as your raise your head you see a clear blue sky above, and feel the gentle healing rays of the sun touch your skin. Breathe in the freshness of a summer meadow. How good it is to be out here in the clear country air!

And now you look down at your feet and see a pathway before you. You decide to follow this pathway, because you know it is the right thing for you to do now. How happy you feel as you walk along this pathway. You know something wonderful is about to happen and you feel relaxed and calm.

Look down at your feet as you follow the pathway. Is it an easy path? Or is it in need of repair? Look at the landscape around you. What colours do you see? You find it easy to remember all the details of what you see.

Now the pathway opens up and you find yourself standing before a magnificent maypole. Look at how high the pole reaches. Does it go all the way up into the blue sky? There are so many coloured ribbons falling down from the pole. Which ones should you choose?

First of all, go to the red ribbon. Look at how bright the red is to your eyes. Feel the redness, and breathe it deep into your body. And as you breathe in the bright red all the way into your body know that your physical energy is being healed.

Now move on to the bright orange ribbon. Look at how bright the orange is. And now breathe in the bright orange deep within and know that your emotions are being unblocked.

The next ribbon hanging down from the maypole is yellow. Breathe in the bright yellow and, as you do so, know that your mental attitude is now becoming bright and positive. There's no room now for darkness. Everywhere is brightness.

Now take the green ribbon in your hand. Feast your eyes on the healing green and breathe it in to your heart. And know now that your heart is being healed.

How wonderfully relaxing it is to be surrounded by the

amazing coloured ribbons of this maypole.

The next ribbon you pick is blue. A lovely bright blue, just like the sky. Now breathe it in, and know that it's now easier to express yourself. Breathe it deep into your throat and feel any blockages are simply dissolving away.

Now you find you have a deep indigo ribbon in your hand. Indigo is like purple and blue mixed together. Breathe in this vibrant colour into your eyes. Know now that the knowledge that comes from within you, your intuition, is now being healed.

The last ribbon you find is pure white. Feel how white and pure it is. Now breathe in that whiteness, all the way into your body and around it. Know that you are always safe and that your entire body is filled with bright new energy. Enjoy this feeling, allow all the energies to course around your body filling you up with newness and lightness.

How healthy and happy you feel now that you have breathed in the red, the orange, the yellow, the green, the blue, the indigo and the white of the ribbons of this maypole.

Now you know that this maypole is your special maypole.

You can choose any or all of these brightly coloured ribbons to bring back with you. See which ones you have chosen. How much brighter the colours seem to you now.

Now you begin your journey back. You leave the maypole behind you.. You find yourself along the path from where you began your journey. It brings you back to your favourite country place.

Breathe in the wonderful scents of summer, feel the warm breeze softly touch your hair, and the gentle rays of the sun touch your skin. How happy and full of energy you feel.

And now I want you to take a deep breath and as you breathe in and out once more you can feel the ground beneath your feet. And now as you breathe in and out again, you can now feel your fingertips. And now as you breathe in and out it's time to open your eyes, and you do so, coming back into this room, feeling relaxed, refreshed and much better than before.

(End of visualisation exercise).

What did you see? The moment you return to consciousness once more use Workpage 1 (p. 35) to write down all you remember

from your meditation. Note the colours you saw around you as you began your journey. Do you remember the state of the pathway: was it cobbled, smooth or rutted, was it a well-beaten track or a tarmacadamed walkway? The state of repair is important because it shows the state of your spiritual path right now. Perhaps the first time you do this you find your pathway is difficult to follow, it could even be full of potholes and broken flagstones. Don't worry if this is the case. It simply means your spiritual health needs looking after, and you've taken the first step along that path today with this exercise.

Which coloured ribbons did you choose? Write the colours down immediately, and any other impressions that you enjoyed during your meditation. Perhaps you saw the maypole ribbons in black and white. If this is the case, it means you are looking at things in your life as only being in black or white, in other words you are not allowing yourself to flow freely. Try to be more open and tolerant, especially with yourself. Allow more colour into your life, be adventurous! If you did see colours were they vivid or murky? Murky colours would suggest that you're not nurturing yourself at the moment, that you need 'polishing up' a bit. Each of the colours that were suggested in the meditation has a particular significance, because they denote the chakras or energy centres affecting various aspects of our life. Our body takes in and sends out energy through our chakras. The chakra colours (which are the same as the colours of the rainbow) are as follows:

Red is the colour of your physical energy and sexuality. If you feel low in physical energy it is a good idea to wear something red. If you usually stay away from this colour, ask yourself are you staying clear of your sexuality? Are you unwilling to move forward in your life? If you find such things difficult, making a conscious decision to have more of this colour in your life will enable you to get moving in these directions.

Orange is the colour of our emotional energy. If you've been through an emotional trauma or some sort, or are feeling emotionally empty, bring some orange into your life. Paint your bedroom peach or orange, or get a poster or picture in this colour for your walls. Or eat more oranges! These small changes in your life can make a lot of difference, and they don't have to cost much money.

Yellow is for our mental energy. You can often feel 'grey' about life or show a very 'sunny' disposition looking at life positively. If you find you are constantly or consistently gloomy, try to surround yourself with yellow. Have you noticed how so many spring flowers are yellow in colour? They certainly do help us to look forward cheerfully to the months ahead.

The colour green is for your heart chakra. When your heart is hurt or you cannot find peace in your life try to spend time in nature. If you can't go to the country spend some time in a park, or just standing on a grass lawn. Should all else fail, buy yourself a pot plant!

Blue is the colour of truth, self-expression and creative energy. I always find it helpful to have something blue within sight when I am giving my workshops or personal readings. If you feel a block when you try to express yourself, wear a blue scarf around your throat which is the area where this chakra is found.

The colour indigo, a mixture of deep purple and deep blue, denotes the area of our psychic or spiritual awareness. The word psychic comes from the Greek word for soul or spirit, 'psyche'.

Often people fear the word psychic, but now you know it simply means spirit. We all have a spirit, so we all have a psychic awareness. If we didn't, our physical body would be dead! It is in this area, the place on the forehead between the eyebrows, that we can find our spiritual chakra and it is from here that we connect with our own spirit and the spiritual world.

White, which is the last colour mentioned in the meditation, is usually the colour given for the crown chakra, which is found on top of our head. White energy comes out of here like a fountain and covers our physical body, even though we possibly cannot see it. The colour white signifies purity, sacredness and protection. This energy keeps our spirit within a protective 'aura' so that we are taking in and giving out energy without losing any or, indeed, without taking in energy – possibly negative – from others.

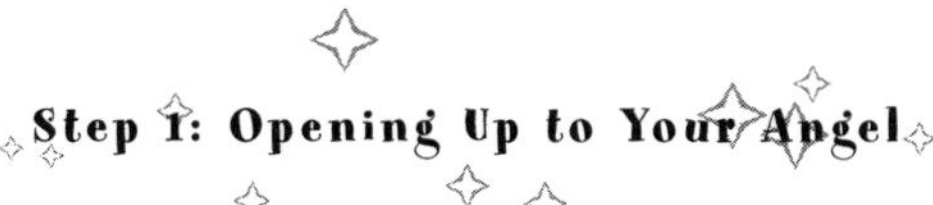

WORKPAGE 1

Date	Colour/s Chosen	The Message

Step 2

Connecting With Your Angel

'Angels speak to those who silence their minds long enough to hear'.

Since beginning my 'Talking With Angels' courses I've been pleasantly surprised at the response of those participating. Some admit, possibly for the first time, that they have heard voices, perhaps seen visions and had experiences which could only have come from their angel friends. I remember one person saying 'This is great, it's the first time I've been able to talk about angels without feeling like an outcast, like I should be taken away by men in white coats!' Others have come to the first class, not knowing quite what brought them there, yet willing to find out more. Though they probably don't realise it at first, they are being prompted by their angels and following their advice.

Angels talk to us in all sorts of ways, all we have to do is be receptive to the chosen form of communication. As you know, I have been clairaudient for many years. Often my angel's voice comes to me during the day, but in more recent years it was more obvious at night-time, when I was asleep. That's really because so often I ignored the day-time voice, thinking I was going plain crazy! It is a gentle male's voice, so insistent that it wakens me up. I have learned to keep a pad and pen handy by my bed so that I can write down the messages I receive. Now that I am working with my angels all the time I don't tend to get so many messages as before. At one time hardly a week went by without some important words being spoken in my left ear and I often received prophetic messages in this way.

One such incident happened to me in the early morning of 4th April, 1994, when I woke up to a heart-broken voice saying 'The President of Rwanda is dead. Rwanda! Rwanda!' I barely knew where Rwanda was, except that it was somewhere in Africa, but I knew this was an important message so I wrote it down and went back to sleep. When I woke up on 6th of April the newsreader related the sad news that the President of Rwanda, along with the President of Burundi, had been killed in an air missile attack while flying to a mutual destination. Since then the lives of the Rwandans have been devastated.

Later in 1994 I was driving home at 11.50pm when a familiar sounding voice came over the car radio. He related in detail all about an aircrash in the Eastern USA in which 135 people, including crew, had died. The voice went on to expand on the area where the plane went down and how difficult it would be to find the wreckage due to the environment and the bad weather the area was suffering at that time. I parked in my driveway and sat listening till the message ended. I remember thinking to myself how calm and well modulated, yet how insistent the newsreader had been. I went into the house and noticed the clock said 11.55pm, and wondered why this broadcast had gone out at such a strange time, instead of waiting for the midnight news. It wasn't until the next morning I realised that the 'news report' I had listened to in my car the night before was relating something that hadn't yet occurred! The accident happened at approximately 8.30pm Eastern USA time, whereas I heard it before midnight Greenwich Mean Time. There is a 4 hour time difference between the two, and I had heard the details about 45 minutes before the aircrash happened. I used to wonder why I was being given messages such as these when it was patently obvious I could do nothing to stop the President of Rwanda being killed or a plane going down in the USA. Now I realise it was just my angels telling me that I can trust the veracity of the messages I am given.

The many communications I have received over the years are not always so dramatic. Often they are just simple messages but very pertinent to me. When I was feeling slightly lacking in confidence in my own decision-making ability a few months ago, I got a very clear message 'Trust comes from within. The only one you need to trust is yourself.' So now I do.

It can be a little frightening to hear a voice speaking directly into your ear without a physical body being attached to it! But it's our ego or conscious self that is frightened by such events,

not our all-knowing spirit. Our spirit is connected with our angels and it knows there is nothing to fear from them for they are our helpers, our friends who we can guarantee will be with us through thick and thin.

Often we can feel unloved and full of fear and it's that fear that stops us connecting with our angel. Fear is the opposite of love. Look at the daily news, look at the situation in our towns and cities. All the problems we see can actually be brought back to fear of some kind: fear of being over-looked therefore we must make ourselves noticed, even in a negative way; fear of loss, so we become inordinately possessive and demanding; fear of losing face so we argue and fight or fear of something we don't understand so we make war with our neighbours.

When we feel unloved in our life we begin to live in fear. Fear manifests in many ways in our personal lives: in feelings of resentment and unforgiveness which stops us loving ourselves and others; in a life of confusion and depression, which keeps us living in the dark; and of course fear also shows up in our physical bodies as dis-ease, which is a symbol of lack of ease in our life.

But it doesn't have to be that way. Because we are loved, we are loved by our angel. Regardless of whether we want it or not, we each have at least one angel close by. You can bring light into your life with the love of your angel, so be open to welcoming your angelic friend into your life now, 'For those who walk with angels shall learn to soar above the clouds.'

Angels want to be our close friends, not some distant formal beings far out of reach. So do treat them as friends. Invite your angel along with you, whatever you are doing, just as you would a friend. Be open. Practise openness every day. Angels are beings of light, so it's a good idea to light a candle for your angel in your home as a conscious decision to invite your angel to be with you. Then, each time you look at the candle flame you will be reminded that you are never alone. And if you drive a car, clear up the passenger seat or the rear seat and make room for your angelic companion.

I have to say, it's great having an angel by my side. I remember a day coming up to Christmas one year I was driving through a particular area of the city which has the name of being less than safe. Unfortunately I got stuck at traffic lights behind a large refuse collection unit and in front of a construction lorry. I had been giving an Angels Course the night before, and one woman said she would clear up her passenger seat so that she could invite her angel to travel along with her in her car. Fortunately for me I decided to do the same thing. For as I waited for the traffic lights to change two young boys came running down an alleyway to my left and, with upraised arms they made for my passenger window as though to smash it. I have always been very fortunate and this sort of incident has never happened to me before. I remember watching the proceedings as though in slow motion with dread. I could almost hear the intake of breath of those other drivers close by who were looking on. Even though I had little to steal, a smashed window would need repair and this was during the time when I was severely 'financially challenged'. Just centimetres from the window the two young boys came to a startling halt, a look of shock and terror crossed their faces, and they raced back up the alleyway without doing any damage to me or my car. What a relief! I don't know precisely what happened, but I firmly believe my angel manifested something or some person in the

passenger seat at that very last moment, hence the boys' looks of shock and terror.

I have also heard of many incidents and read several stories about people being stuck in unsafe situations and being partnered by a figure seen by others but not by themselves. I have no doubt that it is their angel coming to the rescue.

Speaking of unsafe and unsavoury situations, people often enquire why bad things happen in life. Shouldn't the angels be about sorting things out before they get bad? Well, that's an important question. But the answer is that we all have an angel, but we all also have free will. The most notorious criminals and murderers have angels. The difference is, they don't listen to the voice of their angel, they don't open their hearts to their angel's love. Instead of living in the light with their angel they choose to live in the dark, and therefore commit dark deeds. Often we may feel powerless against such negative influences in the world. We might even wonder if there are angels about if so many fearful things can happen, but be assured that whenever you ask an angel to help in a situation, to bring peace and harmony to our land or our planet, our message is received. Our

angels will work for our good, but they really cannot force someone living in the dark to live in the light. So, listen to the advice of your angel. Get out of the way if you feel you are in an unsafe place. Follow through on your 'gut reaction' or 'female instinct'. You can be sure that your inner voice urging action is giving you sound advice, it's connected with your Higher Self, or it's the voice of your angel. Both want only the best for you. While the angels cannot stop someone planting a bomb or driving dangerously, because those people have free will, they can tell us to get to a safe place so that we won't be harmed. So listen and act!

Remember my analogy earlier about everyone being at Earth School? Angels are sent here to guide us through our lives while we're at this school, they are not here to force us into any action. If they were we would never have to learn anything, and that wouldn't be the point of life at all. So no matter who we are or where we live, we have one thing in common, and that is free will. We can ask for guidance and we can reject it. That's our choice. Should we reject guidance our angel will not interfere or force us to do anything, unless our life is actually threatened,

But because they're here to guide us, we must first ASK them for guidance. That's the secret, it's to ASK for help, not PRESUME on help. So how do you ask? You ask just as you would ask a friend for help, such as 'Angel, could you work this problem out for me?' Once you ask, you'll be surprised just how quickly the help comes to you. (And do remember to say 'thanks'.)

Because angels are beings of light they don't actually have names, like we do. They don't live in houses and need telephones or mail boxes in order to communicate. However, we do, and it often seems strange and difficult to talk honestly and sincerely with someone when we don't know their name. So if we ask our angel for its name they will choose one for us, just so that we will find it easier to talk to them as friends, rather than as a nameless stranger. You will probably find it's a name that is recognisable to you. Perhaps the same as someone you care about and love: don't be surprised if the name given is that of your spouse or child. The angels want us to look on them with love and trust, so they often choose a name that fits a loving, trustworthy character in our life. When I first asked my angel its name I thought it had said 'Laura', and my immediate reaction was 'I must have imagined it, that's my niece's name' . Then I saw, in my mind's eye, a line of white squares hanging up like washing on a line, and the letters L-O-R-I-E-L, Loriel, were spelt out for me. (Later I learned that the suffix -el is the old Hebrew word for 'God').

You will get the name of your angel is one of several ways: like me, you might actually hear a name being given. You may see it written down. Or you may just feel a name pop right into your head. Whatever happens, accept the first name that comes into your head, that is the name your angel wishes to be called.

Exercise 3: Naming Your Angel

As they say 'Silence is the language of the Angels', so when you want to connect with your angel do try to find a place of silence. It is always a good idea to light a candle too, which is simply a conscious decision to bring light into your life.

Always begin your meditation by connecting yourself with the Earth as you did in Exercise 1.

When you have done this, simply close your eyes and continue to breathe deeply for a few moments. Try to imagine, as you

breathe in, that you are inhaling golden light into your lungs. Gold is the colour of angels. See it spreading all the way around your body as though it is moving through your blood vessels. As it does so, you are becoming filled with light and therefore finding it easier to connect with your angel.

Now hold your left hand open on your heart. Allow any interfering thoughts to come in and leave your mind, and when you feel you have attained silence simply ask in your mind the question 'Angel, what is your name?' The very first name that occurs to you is the one for your angel.

With your hand still on your heart, ask silently 'Is there anything I need to know right now?' and await a reply. It may come in a spoken message, it may just be a definite feeling you undergo, whichever way it comes it's a message for you at this moment.

What name did you receive? Use Workpage 2 (p. 51) to record the name immediately and also any message you may have received. During the next few days and weeks call your angel by this name and see how close you feel. If it seems completely

unacceptable to you, re-do the exercise and ask again. And remember, you can have more than one angel, so if you get two or three names this means you have two or three angels looking after you.

During one of my workshops, when I came to this exercise I suddenly saw 'Jocelyn' written in sand in my mind's eye. I have since discovered that I have four angels. Loriel who I imagine as my 'Guardian' or 'Companion Angel' and Jocelyn who looks after my business side of things. Then one night I was woken to a voice saying 'My name is Senco'. I didn't know if Senco was a guide or an angel, so I asked and saw Senco standing with angel's wings which immediately began to fade away once I'd noticed them. Senco is a 'get up and get going' type of energy, while Tamara is my Angel of Nature and has a very quiet, gentle energy.

I did have one participant who got the name 'Lucas'. She was disgusted, saying 'But that's the name of car batteries!' However, during the following week she came across several examples of people being called Lucas, including news from a distant relative in Australia who had chosen this name for her newly arrived son. So this can also happen to you; you may at first feel the name you receive has no significance in your life and feel like rejecting it. However, if you keep coming up against the same name understand there is a good reason for this, you are meant to accept it.

Now you have connected with your angel. Your energies have mingled and from this moment on you can begin to transform your life.

Now that you've begun to open your heart to your angel's love, you can transform the way you relate to everyone and everything about you. Begin with everyday things. Angels are here to remind us of the truth, beauty and goodness within everything, no matter how trivial it may seem. If you find you are in a job which you hate, where everything seems lifeless and your career has reached a dead end, take another look at it. If your home is just a building with four walls where you feel no heart connection, or if your neighbourhood seems boring, dull and dreary, look at these things again. This time look at each environment with 'angel eyes'. Search for the beauty and goodness within it and ask your angel to be with you as you do this.

Pause for a moment and look at the machines or implements

WORKPAGE 2

NAMING MY ANGEL DATE

....

....

WHAT I NEED TO KNOW RIGHT NOW: DATE:

....

....

....

....

....

....

....

you use. Do you use them or ab-use them? Do you push your car to its limit and call it names, then wonder why it cuts out on you? Do you shove books or files or tools or food any old how into cupboards or drawers without a thought? Do you walk into a shop and keep your eyes fixed on the product you need at that time and never look around you or connect with the shop assistant? Do you walk by trees and shrubs and flowers and never even glance at their beauty? Why not decide to change and treat every object you use with love and respect whether it's a vacuum cleaner, a computer, a car, a washing machine..? It might sound crazy at first, but though these things may be menial they are all wonderful inventions which make our lives easier. Look on them with angel eyes and when you treat them differently you'll be surprised how they reflect back at you in a lighter, easier way. Your car will become a part of you that brings you on wonderful journeys, your computer will be an amazing extension of your mind, your colleagues will share their energy with you, your neighbourhood will be a living, breathing environment where the plants and trees and flowers bring natural health and beauty into your life.

Once I'd get into a fury if the car or the washing machine or the radio didn't work. Then I began to ask a Technology Angel to sort these things out for me, and it did. Sometimes, of course, I might need a little 'human' help such as if the car battery had run down, but it would always come in a friendly, easy way simply because I'd brought an angel's influence to bear on the problem. I can just imagine my angel sighing and saying 'But Margaret, you only had to ask!'

So do try to look on everything in your life with angel eyes. Invite your angel to be with you whatever you're doing. Whether you're working or playing you'll become more aware of what you're doing, how you're thinking, and what you're seeing. There's no big secret about what words you use to ask for your angel to be with you at these times. Just say 'Angels, please be with me', and they will. Angels are especially helpful when you're facing something you don't want to do, or when you feel you are no good at doing something in particular. Just ask your angel to be with you and you'll find whatever the problem, it will become much easier than you first feared. After all, angels are messengers from God, so no-one would dare overwhelm them!

Angels are everywhere, and the Earth is a gift from God for us to enjoy. Life only becomes a 'vale of tears' when we cannot open our eyes to our angels and their help. Quite often this might be because we are judging ourselves too harshly. Do bear in mind that our angels, those special messengers from God, care for us and guard us day and night, despite any apparent imperfections we might bear, and despite anything we may or may not have done in the past. Also, nowadays we seem to be constantly searching for 'Nirvana', thinking we can reach it if we earn more money, work even harder, wear ourselves out..... etc. It's not necessary for us to be like this at all. Lighten up, bring the light of angels into your life. And have fun! Should you be stuck for guidance on a particular issue or unsure of the right move to make, remember it's simple to find the solution. Simply ask your angel 'Is there anything I need to know right now?' and the answer will be given to you in one of many ways.

Dream Messages

Not everyone is aware that we all get messages of one sort or another while we sleep. Often we discard without thought the

symbols we are shown, saying 'Oh, but it was only a dream'. What a waste! Regardless of whether you remember your dreams or not, we apparently can have up to nine dreams each night. We sleep for approximately eight hours out of every twenty-four. Consider that if we live to be 75 years of age we will each have slept for about 25 years in total during our lives! Just imagine the amount of messages we can receive within that quarter of a century!

The more we record and attempt to interpret the messages we receive, the more easy it will become. If you wish to record your own dreams and try to interpret them, it is imperative that you keep a pen and pad as close to you as possible while you sleep. In this way you will be able to jot down notes from your dream with the least physical effort. Try not to leave dream messages to memory alone. The images can fly away the moment your physical, conscious self comes back to prominence when you awaken. In this way you can miss out on imperative messages.

In ancient times dreams were taken as a normal, everyday, method of being able to communicate with God and the angels. If you are familiar with the Bible you will no doubt have heard

of Jacob's dream of the angels coming down from heaven by means of a ladder, and Daniel being told by an angel in his dream that he would be alright, even though he faced the lion's den when he awoke. Of course there's Joseph's interpretation of the Pharaoh's dreams which had an enormous effect on Egypt through a famine, and in the New Testament not only did Gabriel come to Mary in a dream to tell her she would bear the Son of God, but also Joseph was later warned by Gabriel in a dream to escape from Herod's men.

So often we face such demands during our day that when we go to bed we just want to cut ourselves off from all our cares and we welcome a few hours of oblivion. However, the reason we sleep is so that we can dream. Otherwise, we could simply sit down and rest our bodies after each day, there would be no need for sleep. Dreams help us overcome traumatic events, they give us guidance on what might be coming up in our life, they of course introduce our guides and angels to us. It is very important that we learn to welcome our dream messages. Dream interpretation has been a valid and valued source of spiritual information for many centuries all over the globe. Emperors,

pharaohs, druids ... they've all 'incubated' dreams in order to help their people. In fact, the word incubate comes from the Latin 'incubare', which means 'to sleep on it'. In Celtic times the Druids would look for guidance in their dreams, as did the Japanese Emperor of Shinto religion, when he looked for help for his people. During both the Greek and Roman times temples were built specifically for dreaming, and nowadays when we are faced with a problem we are often advised to 'sleep on it'. It makes sense when you know that, faced with any problem, our spiritual energy can connect with the enormous bank of information that is available from our guides and angels.

If you are looking for the solution to a problem, you can ask your angel to give you help while you dream. The first thing to do is make sure your bedroom is a comfortable, relaxing place to be. Use one drop or two of lavender essence on your pillow at night-time, and if you can try not to listen to the News or see anything violent on television last thing at night. You might like to buy a special notebook you can keep as your Dream Journal. Keep this and a pen very close to your bed, so that you can write down any dream messages you receive with the least possible

physical effort. This is because when we are asleep we are in our unconscious, spiritual self. The moment we awaken we move immediately into our conscious, physical self and it's so easy to lose track of even the most vivid dream on waking. Try the following exercise before you go to sleep. With a little practise it will become second-nature to you.

Exercise 4: Dream Working Exercises

1. Before you go to sleep, make yourself comfortable in your bed. Now tense and relax your feet, and tense and relax your hands. Then say to yourself, or aloud, 'Angel, while I am asleep, please give me guidance on ... (and state the problem). I am open to remembering my dream and interpreting it when I waken.'
2. Bring a small glass of water to bed with you. Drink half of it before going to sleep, while stating in your mind 'When I drink the rest of this water I shall remember my dream'. The important thing here is to remember to finish off the water in the morning!

I am a dream interpreter, and further on I have set out some examples of dreams and their explanations. However, while someone like me can help interpret other's dreams, do be aware that you are the greatest interpreter of your own dreams. Only you know how you felt at the time as you slept, and only you know how you relate to the personality types you see in your dreams. Use the interpretations shown later as a guide to help you, but remember they are not set in stone. As you get into the habit of recording and interpreting your dreams you will become more expert at it. Should you ever have a recurring dream, one that comes to you again and again, this is sending you a very important sign that you are not 'getting the message', which is why it has to be repeated. Once you do 'get the message' that particular dream symbology will cease showing itself to you.

Nowadays we tend to waken to the sound of an alarm or perhaps a clock radio. It is possible that the shock to our sleeping self cancels any dream memory from our mind. It's so disappointing to waken from a lovely dream only to have it vanish the second we open our eyes, and it is virtually impossible to recapture the message. The best way to awaken is, of course, naturally. You can teach yourself to wake up just before the alarm sounds and therefore be able to recall the images of your dream. If you wish to do this, simply put the alarm on for the normal time, say 8am. Then, before going to sleep, see in your mind's eye the hands of the clock or the digital figures showing the time at a few minutes before the alarm is to go off, say 7.57am. You will then waken gently and, before moving your body, run through anything you remember from your dream state. This might not work the first time, but do persevere and you will soon get into the habit of waking in time to 'catch your dream'. Then reach for your pen and Dream Journal and record as much as you can. If all you can remember is a feeling, write that feeling down. It doesn't matter if you record simply a few remembered images, just the act of recording them will get you into the habit of remembering parts of your dreams. Then your angels will be saying 'At last! There's hope that we can send you more messages!'

Unless you live alone your home is probably bombarded by tv in one room, a radio blaring in another, a chat going on somewhere else. Often it seems impossible to find a quiet place in

our lives. It is because we're often unable or unwilling to hear the voice of our angels in our waking state that they come to us with important messages when we are asleep. Over the years I have learned to interpret the messages I receive while asleep and can divide my own dreams into three groups: those which are given by or include my angels, those which are given by my spirit guides, and those which are general messages.

My angel dreams are much more vivid than the others. The colours are brighter than bright and I often see one of my angels within the dream. I remember a dream I had in February 1993. At the time things were not going well for me, and I had just taken on a job writing freelance copy for a magazine. I had no car and there seemed little chance of ever affording one again. Then I had a dream. It was brief but vivid. In it my angel was standing to my right and we were at the back of a red hatchback car. My angel was insisting 'This is for you' and pointing in particular to the small lip at the top of the back window. When I awoke I remembered the dream and knew without a doubt that I would soon own a red hatchback with a lip at the top of the back window. I hadn't a clue what make it would be, so I spent the next few days searching car parks to find this idiosyncrasy. At last I discovered it was a Peugeot 205. Within the month I had been made Editor of the magazine and my income had increased. In this short time I had gone from believing I would never again own a car to searching the newspaper columns for the right one! Then I saw it advertised: Peugeot 205 Hatchback..... It was a reasonably recent model and an affordable price. I rang up the garage and asked the colour. 'Red' the salesman affirmed, and I arranged to take it on a test drive the following day. I had that car more than five years, and called it my 'dream machine' because it has been such a wonderful trouble-free motorcar and, of course, I was given it in my dreams.

Throughout those months I was constantly worrying, most of my fears being based on lack of financial support in my life. As someone said: 'Yesterday is history, tomorrow is speculation. Only today counts.' But at the time I was too wrapped up in negative thinking to even take time to wonder what that meant. One night I woke up with the most, literally, heavenly music playing in my ear. It was as though there was a huge angel choir singing the words 'Celebrate this perfect day' over and over again with descants and all sorts of musical arrangements. I wrote down the message and went back to sleep. For many days I wondered why this music had come to me, with such a simple message. It took time for me to realise that the message was for me alone to say 'Forget tomorrow, forget yesterday. Celebrate this perfect day'. I can still remember how the music went, but I could never attempt to sing it myself. The whole effect was so heavenly.

Another dream I had which I know was sent to me by my angels came about when I had first begun my 'Talking With Angels' workshops. I was still rather shaky in both my finances and my self-esteem, and things seemed to be going rather slowly for me. One night in October of 1994 I had a vivid and memorable dream in which I was handed a huge bouquet of flowers and the next thing I saw was a daffodil right in front of my face. It was as short as that. I knew when I awoke that I was being promised good reason for celebration and congratulation, (the symbol of being handed a bouquet of flowers), and that it would come in the spring, (when the daffodils were out). This kept me going through a bleak winter during which I was con-

stantly asking my angels for help and confirmation that I was doing the right thing. Then in February a journalist came to one of my workshops, asked if she could write an article about me, and the coverage came out in April 1995. The response was phenomenal! It was not until some time later I looked again at my photograph in the magazine. I was sitting at my kitchen table and on it was ... a vase full of daffodils! During that winter which was, to say the least, a 'growth opportunity', I had several dreams of being given banquets, being handed rich chocolate cake, and all sorts of goodies. All these dreams were short, to the point, vivid in colour and totally memorable. A sure sign they were from my angels.

Here are some simple guidelines on interpreting your own dreams:

a. Bear in mind that almost everyone you see, mother/son/teacher/famous personality, etc. is an aspect of your own character. Ask yourself: how would I describe that person to a stranger? Supportive, bad tempered, careless, negative, wasteful, carefree, positive, loving, generous, etc. The dream is about that aspect of yourself.

b. Everyone, whether a man or woman, has both male and female energies. The male energy is that which gets us up and moving, it's the 'doing' energy. The female energy is that which is intuitive, nurturing, the creative and receptive part of yourself. In dreams when we see a man it is often a symbol of our male side, while seeing a woman would symbolise our female energy.

c. Dreaming of someone who dies is not a dream about death. Again, ask yourself, how would you describe that person to a stranger? If you don't think much of the person in the dream, take it as a warning that that aspect of your own character has to die. Or, if you do like that person's traits, the message would be that those traits within yourself are dying, and it's a warning to take care you hold onto them.

d. Should you dream that someone close to you who is aged or ill comes and kisses you or hugs you or simply smiles, this can sometimes warn that this person's spirit is ready to move on and is coming to say 'goodbye'.

e. How you feel in the dream is of paramount importance. I love cats and if I dreamed of them I would feel very content and happy. You might feel ill at ease or downright frightened of them. The message depends on how you relate to the scenes and players within the dream.

f. Each part of the body, each colour, flower, tree and shrub has great significance in a dream. It is imperative that as much of your dream as possible is recorded. It doesn't matter how ridiculous it seems in the clear light of day. The dream came from your unconscious self, so do listen to it.

Some Dream Interpretations

The following are some samples of dreams which hold significant messages for those who are, or are about to be, on the path of transformation.

Dream 1: Papering Over the Cracks

"I was inside a small room of a small house where I had lived when we emigrated first. A very small passage led to another room to my left. Myself and two friends, a female and male, were putting wallpaper up in this room as I watched them. They worked well together, and soon one wall was finished.

But as they began the next wall I noticed that huge blue splodges of paint were coming through the new wallpaper. I said 'Hold on, something has to be done about this', but they ignored me and kept on with their work. The more paper they put up, the more great blue splodges appeared beneath it. I was distraught, knowing that it was just a waste of time 'papering over the cracks'."

The Interpretation: This is a dream I had myself some years ago just before I participated in a very powerful and healing workshop. I was feeling resistance to starting it, and asked for guidance while I slept. The house, small and a place I had lived in some years before, symbolised my small, limited self at that time, who was living in the past. The dream told me that to continue what I was doing would only be 'papering over the cracks' and they would be there for everyone to see, so I might as well stop and re-think what to do. When I awoke I decided to do the workshop. It was a good decision.

Dream 2: Healing Dysfunction

In this dream my client said that it was like being part of the animated tv programme The Simpsons. 'There was plenty of animated action in full colour and, as I watched, the family went underwater in a submarine type machine. Homer Simpson was saying 'Oh no, not all the way down there' but afterwards when they came to the surface, Marge said 'It wasn't bad at all, not half as bad as I thought. I really liked it'. Then a hand came and carried the submarine which looked like a bubble-car, onto the ground surrounding the pool.'

The Interpretation: First of all I would ask myself, what type of family do the Simpsons portray? Even a child could tell you they are the archetypal dysfunctional family. There was a lot of action about and it was colourful, so this suggests that this family keep up some form of action or drama all the time, keeping busy so they rarely have time to stop to look at themselves.

Then they are in an underwater machine and Homer Simpson, the male energy of my client, says 'Oh not, not all the way down there'. Water, especially deep water, is always the symbol of deep emotions. The message is to travel deep into the emotions of her family life, but her male, logical and reasoning energy is saying 'No' to that, he is fearful of being in 'deep water' if he does. But she goes deep into her emotions anyway, and then her female energy, as seen in Marge, says 'It wasn't bad at all, not half as bad as I thought. I really liked it'. So whatever she feared that lay deep within her emotions wasn't half as bad as she feared, in fact she really liked the journey. That's good news and, what's even better, a hand comes down, symbolising help from above, such as help from angels or spiritual guides, which lifts up my client and her many-aspected character, and brings her onto safe, dry land, symbolised by the ground surrounding the swimming pool.

Dream 3: The Image We Portray

At the beginning of his dream my client was wearing tatty clothes in dark colours. He says it looked as though he'd 'been in the wars'. Then he begins to dress in different clothes, but in the dream they are women's clothes, a skirt and a blouse. The skirt was a purplish colour and the blouse a deep pink. He says 'In the dream I was quite happy to be putting them on, they were clean and neat and quite fashionable. But when I

awoke I felt embarrassed and was quite worried to think of how normal they felt! I'm not at all into dressing in women's clothes in reality. I don't have any problems with my sexuality.'

The Interpretation: Often such a dream could remain a secret due to feelings of possible shame and embarrassment. However, my client need have no worries about his feelings in the dream. They were not about changing sex, but instead about projecting a different image to those around him, for clothes represent the person that others see.

The first part of the dream shows him wearing dark, tatty male clothes. What's the image they would represent? That he's showing a dark, bedraggled view of himself to the world. As he says himself, it looked as though he was in the wars. So the dream was saying that his male side that he is showing has been through the wars, and he's probably being too 'macho' about how he portrays himself to others and this is causing him problems because he is not truly being himself. When he shows his female side, as is portrayed by the skirt and blouse, then his life will become calmer and neater, because he'll be more balanced with his male and female energies. The colours are significant: deep purple sig-

nifies spirituality and intuitive power, and pink is the colour of self love.

Dream 4: The Mansion of the Soul

Dream buildings symbolise the whole self, the body and soul. With one exception: if you are actually house hunting at the time of the dream. Often when we visit a building which seems to be our home in our dream, we find there are locked rooms, long corridors, dark stairwells, or beautifully ornate rooms we've never seen before.

In this example my client says he visited this house regularly in his dreams. 'It's completely different from my real home. The house is terraced and looks small from the outside. Some steps lead to the front door. When I come into the house though it's much larger inside, quite rambling, in fact. There's so many rooms that I know I haven't even seen some of them yet. It seems as though I have two or three living rooms, but the people I see in them are strangers to me, like there's a teacher in one, a nurse in another, and someone stacking books along shelves in another.

'When I go to the hallway I see there's a cellar downstairs, but it's dark and I don't want to go down. Instead I go up the stairs and there's a room with the most beautiful pictures on the walls. It's like walking into an art gallery. They're framed in gold frames and the artwork is magnificent. I feel so good looking at them!'

The Interpretation: The dreamer is visiting the Mansion of his Soul, that is his entire self with his hidden potential and his fears as well. The outside of the house, which he sees as a terrace, is how he views himself and how he feels people see him. But inside there are many rooms, symbolising talents and potentials he hasn't yet even looked at. The fact that he has three living rooms suggests he has several different ways of living open to him.

The people in the rooms are significant: they're strangers to him but the message is that these are some talents he hasn't yet realised: the teacher, that's his ability to learn from his intuition, the nurse who is the symbol of his self-healing abilities and the person stacking books, well that sounds like he's building up a library, information he can call on for later reference.

When he goes into the hall he knows there's a cellar downstairs, but it's dark and he doesn't want to go down. The cellar is a symbol of his subconscious desires, especially his sexuality. He's in the dark about this and he doesn't want to investigate further. He may have a fear here, perhaps that he is homosexual or that he may have been hurt sexually and doesn't want to look at this.

In this dream, however, he decides to go upstairs, and this is that he is going up to his spiritual self. When he does so he finds a room like an art gallery: magnificent paintings surrounded by gold frames. That's hidden talents which are framed within his spirituality. The gold frames suggest also connection with his angels.

It would be important for the dreamer to record his current dreams. The reference to the dark cellar where he doesn't wish to explore might suggest that he needs healing regarding his sexuality. If his current dreams contain messages such as being chased by monsters, or being lost, or feelings of being trapped, these could be strong messages to look into his past in this regard.

Dream 5: Sexuality Questions

My client dreamed he was in his home and it was night-time. In reality it wasn't his home, but in the dream it was his home without question. He looked out the back window and saw there were burglars running through his back garden. It seemed as though he could see three men, and they were wearing masks around their eyes. They were wearing black clothes. He felt they would get in through the back way and he ran down the stairs and locked and bolted the back door. He said the door was white, and everything downstairs looked as though it was white. Once he had locked and bolted the back door he felt better, but inside he still felt threatened, and even when he woke up he felt the same.

The Interpretation: As always, the house or home is the person's present state. So this man was feeling that part of himself was being threatened by the equivalent of burglars on the outside. The part of him that was threatened was, in fact, his sexuality. This is because he dreamed he went down the stairs in the dream, and to go downstairs or into the basement is to go either into your subconscious or into your sexuality. It was dark outside, so he felt he was in the dark, because remember every symbol in your dream is a part of yourself. So when he saw the burglars going through his back garden he was actually seeing a part of himself going back into his past. Something happened in this man's past which has seriously affected his present. He feels threatened, as though someone – in the character of strange burglars wearing masks – is coming to steal something from him. Then he runs downstairs and locks and bolts the door, the entrance to his sexuality, and he sees this is white. Everything in his dream is in black and white. That's self-explanatory, that he's seeing things in black and white, not seeing beneath the surface.

The masks that the burglars are wearing are something that he is wearing in reality, masking his true feelings towards his sexuality. When he locks and bolts the door he feels better, but still on waking he feels a residue of being threatened.

The dream is saying that he is not looking at his true sexuality, that he is feeling threatened by it and showing a mask to the world. Something happened to him in the past and he is being advised to go back into the past to see where the problem lies.

Dream 6: Cutting Ties with the Family

Marie was having problems with her family. She was leading her own independent life in Dublin and had begun to realise she needed to heal herself. This would necessitate her going along a rather lonely road for a while, cutting away from the influence of her family who, she knew, meant well, but were very stuck in a rather self-destructive pattern of behaviour of denial. She was voraciously reading books on healing and attending various self-healing courses when she had the following dream.

'I was cycling down a dark road. I knew where I was going, and the darkness didn't bother me because there was light ahead. Suddenly, I almost collided with a tree which had been cut down and was blocking my path. It was a huge tree and I had to get off my bike and skirt around it to get by. The next thing is I'm on a train, alone in a compartment. When I look out I see we're travelling through a forest of fir trees, but they are sparsely planted and there doesn't seem to be much growth, in fact there is snow on the ground in patches.

'The train pulls into what seems like a station and I get out.

Now I am carrying a cat in my arms, almost like a fur wrap, but it is definitely alive. I begin to walk down a pathway through the trees. It is cold, there is a lot of snow about now and I am alone. Although I know I'm going the right way, I am very aware of being alone, apart from the cat which seems to be capable of talking to me. By the way, I love cats!

The Interpretation: Here we have a woman who is making her own way through life under her own steam (symbolised by cycling). Although she seems to be in the dark at present, she can see light in the distance, and she knows she's on the right path. However, her progress is hindered by the tree trunk blocking her path. Trees are a sign of the family tree. This is a big tree trunk, so it could be the male influence (such as her father), or just that her family as a whole is influential in her life. She skirts the block and now she's on a journey led by another, as symbolised by being on a train which is driven by someone else. She's alone at present, except for her Intuition, or her Higher Self, as symbolised by the cat. Cats are very intuitive in reality, and the fact that she is almost 'wearing' this cat seems to me that she is very intuitive and she should trust this ability at all

times because it is, as a cat would be in her eyes, her beloved friend. The landscape of her life at present seems quite barren, and her family (the sparsely situated trees) seems a separate entity in her life right now, she possibly feels isolated from them, as though some coldness has grown between herself and the individual members.

When she completes the current part of her journey which is led by another (such as a healing therapist or group facilitator) she brings her intuitive sense (the cat) with her on her journey. She feels cold and alone. Yet she knows for certain she is on the right path. I like the fact she says it seems like the cat can talk to her, for this is her ability to tune into her intuitive self. It's good that she says she likes cats. If she did not like them in reality and had this type of dream, it might symbolise that she is fearful of her intuitive ability.

Dream 7: The Right Path

Clare was going through a very bad patch in her life when she had this dream. She was unhappy in her job where she worked as a secretary, and wished she could leave, but she was

worried about money. She'd trained as an aroma therapist and was currently beginning a course in reflexology, hoping eventually to set up as a professional offering these therapies. In the meantime she had applied for a job in a different company, again as a secretary.

In the dream Clare was in her workplace. It wasn't quite the same as her workplace in reality. The room was smaller and the paintwork very old and patchy. It was also very dark, although the office was at the top of a building. Clare came into the room and said aloud 'How can I be expected to work here when there's no light?' She said she felt really angry when she saw how dark it was.

Then Clare found herself outside in a field. Part of it was old, burned grass, and she knew that somewhere in the distance the grass would be full of flowers and herbs. She set off on her bike to get there, but the cycling was heavy going. She looked behind her and saw now that she was on a rutted road and discovered she had a puncture in her back wheel. She had to push the bike up a steep hill and when she got to a T-junction she meets someone and they exchange some form of com-

munication. 'I don't know what it was, only that after this I decided to turn right.' Suddenly she was in a field of flowers and herbs, all growing abundantly in direct contrast to the old, burned grass at the beginning. 'I felt so relieved', she says, 'it seemed like a miracle'.

The Interpretation: This dream was all about her career and where she was at present. First of all Clare found her office was too dark to work in, and that was warning her that she would stay in the dark unless she did something about it. The fact she felt angry when she shouted 'How can I be expected to work here in the dark?' was trying to propel her, through her anger, to move out of the dark and into the light. In reality Clare is a very gentle person who often allows others to take charge of her life, so she would probably need to get very angry to get people to hear what she's saying.

Then Clare finds herself in a field. And that's her field of interest in her life at present, in other words her need to have a career change. The grass is old and burned, no good to anyone, in other words. The message here is saying that her 'field of interest', i.e. being a secretary, is gone past it's 'best buy' date as they say, and she's feeling burned out. Somewhere in the distance help is at hand, in the symbol of newly growing herbs, a sign of healing.

The good news is that she's cycling, which means she's going ahead under her own steam, independent of others, which is a very helpful sign, especially as until now she's allowed others to control her life. But she finds the road is rutted and she gets a puncture in her back wheel. So the path she's on at present is difficult, and she is going to suffer a deflation about something in the recent past. I would read that as being a warning that the job she's hoping for isn't for her, and she'll be disappointed. Her dream then had her pushing the bike uphill until she came to a t-junction. Here she meets someone who gives her guidance. It might have been her angel, her spiritual guide, or her higher self. She turned to the right, which suggests she took the right decision on her path in life and suddenly she is in a field of abundantly growing flowers and herbs. 'It seemed like miracle' she says, and that's just what it will be for her, a complete change, after a little deflation, but she will be divinely guided and therefore find herself on the right path in life.

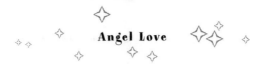

Dream 8: Dream of Pursuit

This is a dream my client has whenever she is anxious. She is a woman in her 30s who is single and running her own business. She's very capable, and very independent with her own home as well. Her dreams were recurring, and getting worse.

> The Dream: *'I'm being chased down narrow streets and know there's no way to escape whatever is coming after me. I'm not sure who it is that's after me, only that it's a man and he's got a knife. I run into a shop doorway, and face the door with my back to the street. I feel that if I can't see my pursuer he won't be able to see me. But all of a sudden I know he's standing behind me and is about to stab me in the back.*

The Interpretation: This is quite a typical 'pursuit dream' where we are being chased by someone or some thing and we know for certain we can't get away, no matter how fast we run. It's an important dream, and it's coming to her again and again, because she hasn't yet 'got the message'. It's telling her that it's time to face herself. This woman is trying to run away from herself. No matter how fast you run, you cannot do this. There's something she won't look at, something she won't face, and it's getting more and more urgent that she does look at it, because the dreams are recurring again and again. The fact that she runs into a shop doorway to get away suggests that she has been given a choice, a place to shop for help. It's right in front of her face, but she doesn't realise it. If she doesn't act quickly she will be stabbed in the back, and the person who will stab her is herself, because she is really being self-destructive by not moving forward on this issue.

Dream 9: The Back Garden

'I was driving up the road to a friend's house. It was nice and sunny. This is a friend who was very good to me when I was vulnerable and helped me a lot. But in more recent times I found out he's not as reliable as I'd thought.

'In the dream I parked outside his house and noticed that the left fender of the car was missing. Although I noticed it, this loss didn't seem all that dramatically important. My friend came to the door and invited me in. The house seemed darker inside than before, and then we were out in his back garden. It wasn't the same as his real garden. All that was there were row

upon row of apple trees. They were out in blossom but the entire garden was just covered in a thick layer of snow. We stood there, not saying anything. I felt very sad. Then the dream ended.'

The Interpretation: Here is an example of a dream which is about someone other than the dreamer. This dream is about a change in the way this woman feels about not only this particular male friend, but about herself. Earlier she had found that there was a lot of growth in her life when she was in contact with this man. She's driving a car, which is a good sign, because it means she's making her own way through life. However, as she says, the fender is missing on the left. Well, the fender is the symbol of a de-fender, and this is saying her female defence is down, she's very vulnerable and has probably put too much trust and dependency on this male friend. Instead, she should have relied on her own 'male' defences.

When she goes into the house she finds it's much darker than usual, so it seems like the light has gone out of this relationship. Then they go into the back garden, which symbolises something going on in the past. Apple trees are a sign of knowledge and nourishment. They can also be a symbol of sexual temptation. In Celtic times they symbolised magic. So the knowledge and magic that she believed in the past was to be found with this man has now been covered in snow. In other words, it's frozen and unable to grow. I also feel that perhaps the two were tempted at some point to carry the relationship further but a coldness descended before they acted upon it.

The message here is that there is no magic in this relationship any more,. She should look after her inner defence system, in other words her intuitive sense, and listen to its messages. She says she felt sad standing there. Something she really believed in has come to an end and it's natural to feel a sense of loss about it.

Dream 10: Warning of a Coming Death

As mentioned before, to dream of a coffin, or of someone being buried is not a warning of physical death, but a warning that some part of you is dying away. No matter how often I tell people this, it is very difficult for the dreamer to believe it! However, we can be warned of death in our dreams and I am

now going to relate three specific dreams I had which warned me of deaths I would have to face in the near future. I hope this can help you understand the difference of having a dream in which you *see a death*, and having a dream which is *about a death*.

Dream a): I wanted to know if Jim, a friend who was terminally ill, would die within a week as I had some travel plans which would have to be changed if I needed to go to his funeral. At this time Jim was suffering from bowel cancer and was being cared for in a hospice. He had several kilos in weight and looked a lot older than his 40 years. As I was going to sleep I simply asked my angel to let me know what the current situation was.

> *In this dream I saw Jim looking very young, and healthy. There was not a trace of pain or illness to be seen. His skin had colour and he was happy, smiling and laughing. Although I only saw his face, it felt as though he was at a party and having a lot of fun.*

The Interpretation: On waking the next morning, I knew that he had died. He was no longer in pain, he had no more worries.

Later that day I received a phone call that confirmed what I already knew because of my dream.

Dream b): *My Mum, who was in her 90th year, had been infirm for several years and was being cared for in a nursing home. Over the years we had almost lost her several times, but on 31 July 2002 I dreamt that I was in my kitchen in my last home on North Circular Road, looking out of the window of my kitchen over the back garden. There was a wooden chair by the window and when I looked at it I saw that the back support of the chair was broken and pink liquid was gently flowing out of the part where it was broken. In the dream I was devastated as I saw this. When I awoke I felt my heart was broken because I knew this was a warning of my mother's death.*

The Interpretation: My old home is the symbol of my past. 'North' is going to spirit, 'Circular' is the circle of life, death and rebirth, and 'Road' is the pathway we take. The back garden is how things used to grow in the past. The kitchen is the place of nurture and nourishment. The window is the barrier between the present and the past, we can look through a window and see

the past, but not touch it still. The chair is the sign of support, and who is the most supportive person in your past? Most likely your mother! The support part of the chair was broken, was not able to support me any more. The pink liquid symbolises unconditional love, something that a parent gives you. Most of all, the feeling I had gave me the greatest clue. I felt utterly devastated in the dream, I knew there was nothing I could do to repair that chair, and when I awoke I knew it was an advance warning about Mum. She passed away peacefully in her sleep less than three weeks later. During the night she died I had a very quick vision of her as a young woman. I knew on waking that she had left. Though it hurt I was grateful to have been warned in advance and glad for her that she was happy and well again.

Dream c): Many years ago I had had a horrible, painful experience of euthanasia with my previous pet, Leo. I dreaded, as all pet lovers do, the idea of either of my present pets needing to go through the same thing. More recently, one of my cats, Zaggy, who at that time was 18 years old, developed cancer. She

slept mostly and ate little, but purred a lot and was very content. Then one night she began to breathe with difficulty. As the night went on she couldn't settle. I knew this was it, I had to do something. I had been saying to her that it was alright for her to go, and thanked her for all the years together. I asked my guides and angels to please give me a clear message to make me certain I was right to call the vet. I slept literally for about two minutes and in that short time I had a vivid dream.

The Dream: *It lasted seconds but was simple and clear: I was approaching the top of an escalator and though I couldn't see who it was, I knew I was holding the hand of someone I cared about. The moving staircase was coming to its destination and all I could see was a very bright, inviting light. In the dream I felt safe and calm. I knew I was doing the right thing.*

The Interpretation: On waking I knew I needed to 'offer a helping hand' to Zaggy. That morning the vet came and gave Zaggy an injection. Zaggy had always been very nervous, (especially of vets!) but in this instance she seemed to welcome her. In a moment or two she had gone peacefully. I went to bed shortly after the vet left and, as I closed my eyes, I had a vision of Zaggy as a young, lively, healthy cat, lying on her back, playing with butterflies in the air. It was so unexpected! Though I was devastated by what had just happened, I knew without a doubt it was a very clear, loving message of 'thanks' from her to me for allowing her to be released and be free.

There's an addendum to this story: A few weeks later I wrote about the above experience to someone who was going through a similar situation, and that night I had a most wonderful dream/vision. My other cat, Ziggy, sleeps on the bed with me, and I woke in the middle of the night with the feeling of a cat jumping lightly onto me. The thing that really woke me was the loud purr. It was *so loud*! When I looked it was Zaggy, she was well and so happy and she and her sister Ziggy were rubbing against each other and purring. I said 'Zaggy, I thought you were dead!' and she came and rubbed her face against me, as though she was smiling, and just purred. I know this was more than just a dream and I was so grateful for her visit. Although it still hurts to have lost her I know for certain she is still around. And even more important, happy and well.

Dream 11: The Neglected Child

Whenever you dream of anyone it is always the symbol of yourself. Dreaming of an infant or a child is a message about your own 'inner child'. Everyone, no matter what our age, has an 'inner child', the part of us which at a very young age faces some type of trauma and, because we do not have the ability of reason or logic at that young age, we get the wrong impression about life at that time and it can affect our emotional growth detrimentally. (Now you know why adults often 'act like children'!)

The Dream: *I was in a bright new kitchen, everything was clean and it seemed unused. I felt really enthusiastic and I seemed to be busy, though I'm not sure what I was doing precisely. Then all of a sudden I noticed there was a baby right in front of me. I knew I'd forgotten to change or feed her. I got such a shock, what a terrible mother I was! And how had I managed to forget about her? That woke me up with a jolt.*

The Interpretation: This is quite a common dream when we are at a point of major change in our lives. I knew Suzanne as she had come to some of my workshops. She was very interested in the spiritual aspect of life, but often let 'life' take over and distract her. Suzanne was single and had no children, so why did she dream about a baby? It was, of course, a message to look after what had been recently new born in her life. The kitchen is the place of nurturing. It was new, bright and seemed unused, so Suzanne was at a point in her life when she was being given the chance to start afresh, looking after her emotional needs. She's enthusiastic about this chance, but is busy doing something that's not important enough to be worthy of note. In other words, she's being distracted from doing what she is meant to. The baby is in front of her, and that's what is facing her at that time in her life. She needs to look after the baby, the new beginning in her life. Suzanne should stop keeping 'busy' and start nurturing herself by helping her newly discovered spiritual side develop and grow.

Dream 12: The Green Light

I'd like to finish this section on dreams by describing one I had myself recently. There were many changes in my life at this time. I had begun to take my workshops abroad, I had changed my publisher and generally was taking more responsibility for my career, planning ahead and being very pro-active, rather than waiting for others to suggest things to me. Although I trust totally in the angels I did wonder on occasion if I was doing the right thing.

The Dream: *I was cycling along a roadway in a town or city. Someone was to my right side, in the dream it seemed like a friend, someone trustworthy and calm. I could see office buildings and shops on either side of the road, which was quite wide. It was nice weather: sunny with just a few clouds in the sky. The road was straight and while it was busy with other traffic it wasn't congested. Each time I approached a set of traffic lights they would be red, and I wondered if I'd be able to brake successfully. But as I came nearer to them they would automatically turn green. I didn't have to put the brake on even once, just kept moving forward without any hindrances.*

The Interpretation: Any vehicle symbolises how you move in your life and also your motivation. To cycle is to be in total control of your journey, moving forward under your own power. The person to my right, accompanying me on my journey and helping to keep me calm, I believe was my angel. A town or city

is a place of choices. The roadway is the path you are taking. The weather was clement, not stormy or cold. The traffic lights tell us when to go ahead and when to stop. My fear of whether I could brake in time was saying I was uncertain if I should go ahead with my plans or stop. As the lights always turned green on my approach, it looks like the way ahead is clear! This is a far cry from Dream No. 1 above, where there was a great need to paper over the cracks! I'm very glad I looked at them now.

There are many books available on interpreting your dreams. If you are open to learning more about them, I would suggest 'The Dreamers Workbook' by Nerys Dee, published by Sterling Publishing, USA (1990) and Aquarian Press, UK (1989), Dream Dictionary by Tony Crisp, published by Optima (1990) and Pocketful of Dreams by Denise Linn, Triple Five Publications, (1988), Australia. However, while using such books as a guide, do remember to listen to your own intuition, because they are your dreams, no-one else's. Don't forget to check out how you *feel* in the dream, and also how you feel on waking. Now, start recording your dream messages, no matter how unimportant they seem to you just now. The more you record them the more

likely you are to be able to tune into this unique form of healing from our angels, guides and our own spirit which does not cost us a cent!

Step 3:
Forgiving and Letting Go

'Walk in the presence of angels,
for those who walk with angels learn to soar
above the clouds.'

Now that you have taken the first step in connecting with your angel, it's right for you to spend some time together. Often we fear we do not deserve an angel because of something we did or said in the past, or perhaps we're holding onto a belief that we should have done or said something and now we're carrying a burden of guilt that's holding us back from this angelic connection. Just bear in mind that you're

still at school. You're on 'a learning curve' as they say nowadays and when you're still a learner it's okay to make errors now and again. (Just learn from them!)

As the saying goes 'Angels fly high 'cos they take themselves lightly'. They don't carry burdens of the past or the possible future with them. They do not judge us. They live in the ***now,*** in the present. Yesterday does not exist, nor does tomorrow. It is just this present moment. This is how we should live. What is the point of holding on to past hurts and guilt? Does it make you any better? If you are holding onto anger about someone, does it make that person improve? Think about it for a moment. Think of the effect holding onto any anger or resentment has had on your life.

I vividly remember one participant in a workshop telling me how she had held onto anger and bitterness about something someone had said to her some years before. This feeling of anger and resentment had, she realised, coloured (or, to be more accurate, dis-coloured) her life for many years. Finally she met this person again and faced him with the pain she had been carrying. The final insult, she admitted, was that he didn't even

remember her! Fortunately this woman had undergone a lot of healing in recent times, so she was able to see the funny side of the situation she had built around herself, and also how pointless and self-destructive her mind-set had proven to be. But, as she pointed out wistfully, 'Those wasted years!'

If we truly want to open our hearts to angel love it is essential that we at least try to be willing to forgive. Angels forgive us, don't they? No matter how big or small the situation, we must at least try to be willing to forgive. There is no way we can overlook our unforgiveness if we really wish to connect with our angels. As Jesus Christ said 'Judge not, that you will not be judged.' Nobody is perfect, not even me! We're not meant to be, that's why we're here on Earth School.

If you have been having a hard life so far, what lessons have you been offered? What have you learned from them? I know only too well how difficult it is to let go and forgive, but believe me it's only self-destructive to hold onto anger and unforgiveness. Apart from physical dis-eases these burdens can give you, your spirit cannot be free if it is being held back in the darkness of unloving energies. Do you really want to have resentment growing inside you like a cancer, or bitterness causing you ulcers? When you look at incidents in your life, the negative and painful ones, ask yourself 'What lesson should I have learned from this?' It will really change your perception of such incidents and, when you realise you have learned from them, help you to move forward quite dramatically.

Over the years I have come to understand that my life and the people in it is a reflection of myself. If someone is being judgemental about me, how am I judging others? If someone is showing me lack of support, do I support others? If someone hasn't paid me for work, have I kept payment back from others? These are the questions I must ask myself when faced with a problem. There is a universal law called 'The Law of Ten-Fold Return'. Whatever I give out I know I shall get back ten-fold. Let's say I offer a free reading or a free place on my workshop to someone who is in need. I possibly won't get my fee back ten times over from that person, but it is likely that I will be offered something free from some other source or, as has often happened, that person who was in need accepted my offer and then recommended me to other people who in turn recommended...... etc. That's the good news. Of course, the Law of Ten Fold Return also works on negative energies. Let's say I criticise someone. It is a guaranteed fact that I, in turn, will be criticised by someone within a very short time, and it will be ten times worse than the criticism I gave out! If for no other reason than simple selfishness, do remember this Law of Ten-Fold Return. It is a Law and nothing can change it.

When I feel like criticising someone (as I said, I'm not perfect!) I try to remember that each of us has a diamond within us. The diamond is a symbol of the many facets of our being, our spirit, our love, our aspirations. This diamond may not yet be sparkling on all fronts, in fact most of its facets might be in dire need of a good clean, but I know without a doubt that there is this diamond within each of us. When someone has been on the road of self-healing, their diamond brightness shines out of their eyes and out of everything they do. It's wonderful to spend time with such people because they spread their shining brightness all around them.

Often the person you are learning a lesson with at this moment may seem to be without any diamond brightness what-

soever. Difficult though it may seem, when I am faced with such a situation, I try to imagine that I see either their shining diamond within or else their angel beside them, because I know without a shadow of a doubt that they do have an angel. If we could all see angels at all times can you imagine how differently we would act? My attitude towards these people then changes accordingly. (Though I have to admit it often is not easy, but it does work.)

Because we are all still students on this Earth, we must each learn our own lessons. That means, although you might be watching someone you love being in trouble, you should only support them, not take the trouble away from them. The 'trouble' is a lesson that must be learned. Think of it this way: if you have a child going to school and you do his or her homework, when it comes to exam time, what will happen? Most likely the child will fail, because no lesson has been learned, and so the same test or exam will come up again and again until the student has learned the lesson.

Do you really want to see that happening to someone you love? Instead, support the person going through the lesson.

Offer advice, but allow the person to learn the lesson. Give unconditional love and support. In that way the test will be passed and, just like at school, the same test will never have to be re-sat. When you pass the 'test' you'll find how true this is. No matter how much energy a problem has taken up in your life, whether it's about money, relationships, self esteem.... when you learn the lesson you find that this 'problem' just seems to fade away into the mists of time. Looking back you will ask yourself did it really influence your life so drastically? It will seem like a dream.

We are rarely aware of the power of our thoughts and our words. Think of the figure 8, the symbol of infinity. If I think or say something about someone or some belief in my life, that intent will be sent outwards from me into the Universe and, like the figure 8, it will return to me in some way. We can use that power of the spoken or written word to good effect in our lives, with some very simple exercises.

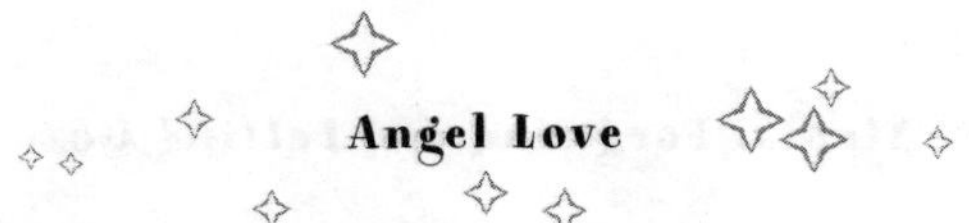

Exercise 5: Angel Connections

If there is someone in your life who is facing problems, there is a very simple way of helping them out without interfering. Simply connect with their angel. There are two ways of doing this:

Find some quiet space and go within yourself. Ask your angel to talk to their angel and sort something out, help them be more aware of choices, etc. Or talk to their angel directly. You don't have to know its name, just the very intention of connecting with their angel means you are in contact. Ask for help on their behalf, then step back and let the person learn the lesson with the help from their angel. It doesn't matter if the person in question believes in angels or not, their angel is there for them. Situations and opportunities will be synchronised for their learning.

Another way of connecting is through the written word. The Chinese believed that every written word had a power of its own, and so would not destroy any written material. When we put something in writing we really emphasise our intent. We can use this power to connect with angels.

Again, find some quiet space and either use Workpage 3 (p. 107) to write a letter to this person's angel. It's as simple as that! Just begin 'Dear Margaret's Angel....' or similar. It's important to remember that we must try not to manipulate any situation. The person who we care for has to learn the lesson, we cannot do it for them. So couch your letter or spoken request in general terms such as 'Please help ...(name).... discover the perfect outcome.....' Or 'Please show ....(name).. the perfect way...' and leave the rest to the angels. Do remember to give your thanks as well.

When we are stuck in our life or finding situations or relationships difficult, we can use the same method of angel connection to help ourselves. Just ask your angel to put you on the right path, again in written word or in spoken word. Or, should the situation seem really insurmountable in your eyes, you might find it more supportive to do both! Examples might be 'Dear Angel (Name if you know it), Please help me to move on from this (relationship/job/ problem, etc.) in the perfect way. Thank you.'

The important thing to remember after doing such exercises

is to STAND BACK and let the angels do the work. Train yourself not to interfere, no matter how hard it might seem to keep your distance. You have asked for angelic help and you know for certain that it's on its way. Don't meddle, no matter how nerve-wracking it may seem at the time! It will all come about in the perfect way, in what's known as 'angel time'. It is man who invented horology, that is time divided into seconds, minutes and hours. Angels live in the now, which is neither the past nor the future. They will bring each of us to perfect understanding in angel time, which is the perfect time for us.

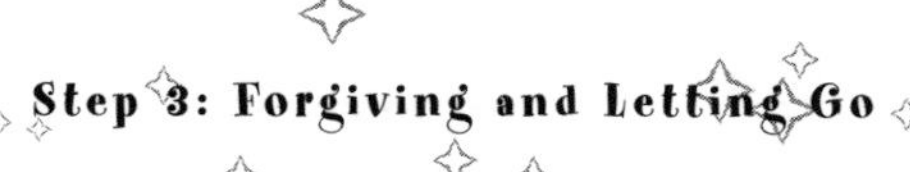

WORKPAGE 3

ANGEL LETTER WRITING Date ....

Dear ....

....

....

....

....

....

....

....

....

....

As I believe that we have each chosen our life in order to learn lessons along the path to enlightenment, therefore we have chosen our family, our country, our race, our tradition, our culture. Each choice has been made so that we will be offered certain lessons in our life. It is imperative that we take responsibility for our choices and recognise that if we are faced with problems the answer is to learn the necessary lessons from them. Blaming our father, mother, sister, brother, school teacher, country, religion, the weather, etc etc for any lack in our life gets us absolutely nowhere. It is just a sign that we are unwilling to open up to the fact that we are spiritual beings who require enlightenment. Working on this assumption, it is important that we look at each relationship in our life and see if there is a lesson to be learned from it. The major lesson we are all learning, of course, is to show unconditional love, which is what God, our angels and our guides show us. It's easy to say this but not always so easy to live this!

If you recognise that you chose certain people in your life, it is only sense that you learn the lesson, the need for unconditional love, from it. The lesson has then been learned and you

can move on. And the moving on will bring great joy, peace, harmony and abundance into your life. Many people have suffered greatly at others' hands often through physical, sexual and emotional abuse, violence, manipulation and even murder. Whatever the suffering. the lesson required is still to show unconditional love, though it may seem virtually impossible.

Often in our relationships we put all sorts of qualities of perfection onto people, place them firmly on a pedestal and then when they show their human imperfections, in other words topple from this pedestal, we accuse them of letting us down, being less than perfect, etc. Who said they were perfect in the first place? Chances are it was us! The lesson here would be to free ourselves from the need to manipulate others into being the people we want them to be. Allow that person to be free. We can then cut the ties that are binding us, the 'tie' being the lesson we need to learn in such relationships.

Exercise 6: Forgiving

When faced with one such a situation, say the following when you think of the person:

'I forgive you for not being as I wanted you to be,
I forgive you and I set you free.'

In this way you are allowing them to be free from your conditional expectations and, very importantly, freeing yourself from the lesson you needed to learn. It is a truly freeing experience to let go of judgement and pre-conceptions about people!

Another little phrase which is extremely effective is to say either in your head or aloud:

'The Light within me salutes the Light within you.'

This is allowing your Higher Self and the Higher Self of the other person to connect. Gone, then, is the human hurt and lack of love. This is another form of unconditional love, this time connected through our spiritual aspect.

If you find that a memory of a person or hurt keeps revolving around your mind, no matter how much you try to free yourself from it, say the following several times a day:

'Love, light and wisdom.'

Although it seems almost too easy, these small words will begin to reprogramme your memory so that what you have in your life is 'love, light and wisdom' rather than anger, fear, agression, pain.......... etc.

Often it seems impossible to get out of fiery, angry relationships. If you know that you are going to meet someone with whom you have 'a growth opportunity', (otherwise known as 'a problem'!), you can ask your angel to intervene on your behalf to help you in the situation. In fact, better still, you can connect with the other person's angel and ask for help from that direction too. Simply say to your angel 'Angel, please help me react lovingly to ......' And 'Can you please connect with ....'s angel and help sort out our problem before we meet?' You will find that something will be different when you both connect. However, it might not be all 'love and light' as you may have wished when you asked for help, but that doesn't mean your angels did not intervene. It may be obvious to them that you

need to do something yourself in order to heal the relationship. Sometimes we must face a situation, accept it exists, then let it go. It's often the acceptance and letting go that prove to be the difficulty for us, but that would be the lesson to be learned. If our angels smoothed out our passage through life without us even knowing that problems existed, then we would never learn any lessons. So sometimes you may find that you ask your angel for help and the situation appears to get worse rather than better! No, it's not that your angel has ignored you, it's just that your angel knows what's best for you in this instance and perhaps you have to be brave and face something you'd prefer to ignore. Difficult though it may be, remember your angel is right beside you and, the instant you learn the lesson, it tends to almost immediately disappear. So, my advice is .... go for it, with your angel's help.

It is also possible to send healing to someone who has passed onto the next life. Through several different channels I have had it confirmed that the 'essence' or 'spirit' in the other dimension is grateful for all the help it receives from this world. Often the tie that binds us, the lack of forgiveness that we feel towards one another, can keep us from evolving in the journey of enlightenment. It is a wonderful thing to send forgiveness and understanding onwards. And have no fear, no 'ghostly spirit' will come and haunt you! Quite the opposite, it is more likely you will have a wonderful dream in which you are thanked for your generosity of heart. And, as an added bonus, you will feel a freedom within yourself that you have not felt before, because you are now free from the imprisoning bonds which may have been keeping you from moving onwards and upwards.

If you wish to send healing and forgiveness to someone who has passed on, simply think of that person as you knew him or her, then say the words as shown above, such as 'I forgive you for not being as I wanted you to be, I forgive you and I set you free'.

Exercise 7: Writing It Out

We can use our own writing ability to help heal our relationships. You don't have to have any special training to do so, it's just like writing a note to a friend.

Use Workpage 4 (p.115) to write your letter to your angel. It's as simple as in Workpage 3 .

Again, try not to manipulate a situation. Leave it open for the best possible good to come out of it. Perhaps it might be useful to ask for 'the perfect outcome' for whatever the problem is. Again, bear in mind that sometimes what is 'perfect' on the path to enlightenment might not be quite so 'perfect' for our human emotions. However, trust that your angel is here to help.

Just write 'Dear Angel' or 'Dear ....'s Angel' and continue in your own words. No big words are required to impress. Just keep it simple. Start at the beginning.... and go on to the end. And don't forget to date the letter. It really will open your eyes to your angel's love when you begin to realise just how easily and quickly your requests are answered. Be very aware that you shall get what you ask for, so make absolutely sure that you want those things in your life. For instance, if you're looking for a romantic partner, bear in mind that if you simply ask for 'a man' for instance, you will get one, but possibly a man who might be an alcoholic, a down and out, a violent person, etc. So do phrase your request as 'the perfect man for me right now' or whatever words are appropriate.

In case you are feeling a lack of love in your life, you can also write to the Angel of Love and ask for love to be sent to you, in the perfect way. Then........ be open to receiving it!

WORKPAGE 4

ANGEL LETTER WRITING 2 Date................

Dear .Angel

....

....

....

....

....

....

....

....

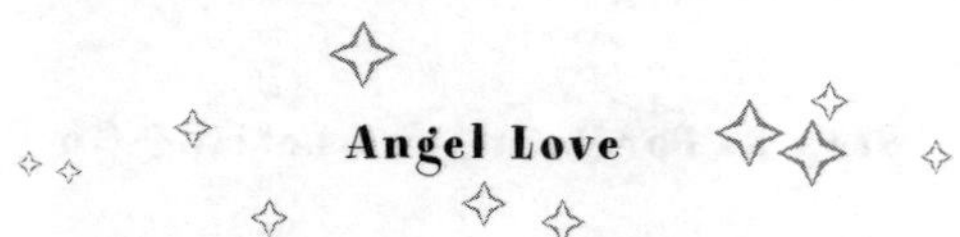

Exercise 8: Flowers of Forgiveness

The following guided visualisation exercise will help you heal relationships. Try it as often as you feel is necessary to heal as many relationships as you wish. Again, follow the steps in Exercise 2 regarding recording the visualisation, and remember to ground yourself first (Exercise 1).

When you're in a comfortable position, take a deep breath and as you breathe in imagine there's a beautiful white light travelling up your toes, across your feet and into your ankles, and as you breathe out allow any tension in this area to gently flow out into the ground below.

Now as you breathe in, the beautiful white light travels up from your ankles into your calves, and moves up into your knees. And as you breathe out allow any tension in this area to gently flow out into the ground below.

Now breathe in the white light and feel it rise into your upper torso. See the white light travel into your heart and into your lungs. And now it moves up into your shoulders. And as you breathe out allow any tension in this area to gently flow out into the ground below.

And as you breathe in, the beautiful white light travels all around your shoulders, releasing any knots and tension there. It flows gently down into your upper arms, your lower arms, and into your finger tips. And as you breathe out any tension in this area gently flows down into the ground below.

Now breathe in the beautiful white light up into your throat and into your neck. The white light releases any blocks in your throat and you find it easier to express yourself creatively. And now the white light moves up into the back of your head, And as you exhale any tension here gently flows out into the ground below.

Watch as the white light moves up into your ears, and it moves into your chin and your mouth, into your nose, up into your eyes and your forehead and now it goes all the way under your scalp and up to the crown of your head. And as you breathe out any tension here gently flows into the ground below. And you know that the Earth will recycle anything you have exhaled and turn it into light.

You know now that you are filled from the tips of your toes

to the top of your head with pure white healing light. And as you gently breathe in and out you feel healing take place all over your body, and in particular in any place where there is a blockage of energy. How wonderful it is to be filled with healing white light. How happy and content you feel!

Now I want you to imagine that you are in a country place, standing on the top of a small hill. As you look around you you see that far in the distance are mountain peaks. What a beautiful sight they are. And now you look below and see a green valley. How relaxing the green seems, and how quiet it is. All you can hear is bird song and the sound of my voice. You feel completely relaxed and at peace as you look around you. And as your raise your head you see a clear blue sky above, and feel the gentle healing rays of the sun touch your skin. Breathe in the freshness of the country air. How good it feels!

And now you look down at your feet and see a pathway before you. You decide to follow this pathway, because you know it is the right thing for you to do now. How happy you feel as you walk along this pathway. You know something wonderful is about to happen and you feel relaxed and calm.

As you move down, down, down into the valley, you breathe in the green of the countryside around you. And with each breath you know that you are renewing your energy and beginning to heal your heart.

Now you find yourself in a field of flowers. It must be the most beautiful field of flowers that ever existed! Just look at the wonderful colours! Look at their beauty! It feels so good to be in this field, absolutely surrounded by flowers. Breathe in their beauty, deep into your heart. You are filled with a sense of serenity, of inner healing. As you stand in this field you realise that you have been joined by your angel. Your know your angel loves you and has come here to help you heal. You see your angel reach down and pick a magnificent flower. Your angel now hands you this blossom. Accept it, it is a gift from your angel and a gift from nature.

Look at the blossom. See its beauty and its colour. Drink it in with your eyes. And as you do so know that your sense of sight is now being healed.

Now bring the blossom to your nose, and breathe in its perfume. And as you breathe in its perfume you know that

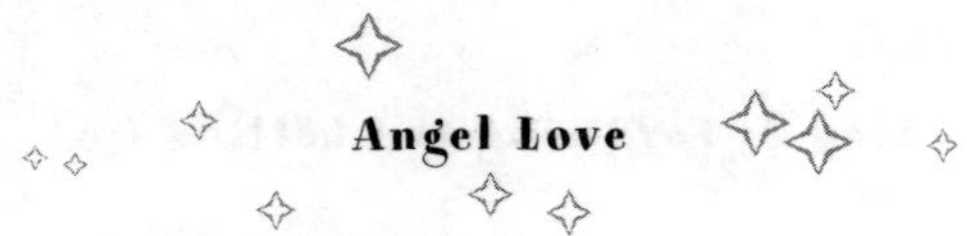

your sense of smell is now being healed.

Take the blossom and place it gently by your ear. Listen, as its petals quietly unfold. And as you listen to its gentle movement, know that your sense of hearing is now being healed.

Now carefully place your fingertips on the blossom and feel the delicate petals. How soft and gentle they feel under your fingertips. And as you enjoy the touch of the petals you now know that your sense of touch is being healed.

Carefully take one petal into your fingers and place it on your tongue. As you swallow allow the taste of this petal to enter your taste buds. As you swallow realise how delicious it is! And know that your sense of taste and your taste for life, is now being healed.

Now understand that your angel wants to help you heal a relationship. To heal a relationship with someone who is in your life at present. Invite this person to come and join you in this field of flowers. Watch as this person approaches. You understand that the reason you have met this person is to learn a lesson between you. What could that lesson be? Accept the first idea that pops into your head.

Your angel now picks another flower and hands it to you. Now offer this person the gift of a flower as a sign of healing your relationship. See yourself passing this flower to the person and watch their reaction. Know that, whatever happens, you have done your part of the healing process regarding this relationship.

Now your angel wants to help you heal a relationship with someone who you may not have seen for some time. Invite this person to join you in this field of flowers. Watch this person coming towards you. You understand that the reason you have met this person is to learn a lesson between you. What could that lesson be? Accept the first idea that pops into your head.

Your angel now picks another flower and hands it to you. Now offer this person the gift of a flower as a sign of healing your relationship. See yourself passing this flower to the person and watch their reaction. Know that, whatever happened, you have done your part of the healing process regarding this relationship.

Now your angel wants to help you heal a relationship with someone who has passed on to the next life. You know that the person's essence will welcome this healing which can help on the journey of evolving. Invite this person to join you in this field of flowers. Watch this person coming towards you. You understand that the reason you met this person was to learn a lesson between you. What could that lesson have been? Accept the first idea that pops into your head.

Your angel now picks another flower and hands it to you. Now offer this person the gift of a flower as a sign of healing your relationship. See yourself passing this flower to the person and watch their reaction. Know that, whatever happens, you have done your part of the healing process regarding this relationship.

It's time to leave this magnificent field of flowers now. Thank your angel for being with you, as always, and for the gift of the blossoms. Find yourself back once more in the valley. See how bright the colours seem. How fresh the air smells. How joyful the birdsong is in your ears!

Now you move out of the valley and begin to climb up, up, up, up to the hilltop from where you started this journey. Now you have reached the top and you realise it's time to return to this room. So take a deep breath and as you breathe in and out, you feel once more the ground beneath your feet. Now breathe in and out again, and this time feel your fingertips. And now it's time to breathe in and out once more, and this time you know you are to open your eyes, returning to this room, feeling relaxed, refreshed and much better than before.

Everything you see in these Visualisations has its own symbology or meaning. Use Workpage 5 (p. 126) to record your experiences. Do you know the name of the flower or was it one you imagined? Do you know if it has any healing properties? Rosemary or Forget Me Not, for instance, would suggest that you should remember these people with love and understanding, rather than negative memories. Roses are for intimacy and love. Roses, of course, are nowadays the symbol of St Valentine's Day, or love that is not yet openly declared. A snowdrop, daffodil or crocus would suggest a new beginning as they blossom in Spring. A water lily suggests growth and beauty in the emotional life (water being the symbol of emotions). Carnations are for trust and fidelity, lilies for steadfastness, honeysuckle for constancy, marigolds for wisdom and violets for patience and hope.

Do you remember the colour of the flowers? If you wonder what each colour signifies, refer back to page 31. Were the flowers that you handed to each person different or the same? Remember to keep a record on the Workpage 5. Ask yourself how you would relate to the flower that you saw and if they have a specific meaning. Certain flowers would have appeared because of how you relate to them.

What lessons have you learned? Have there been power struggles in your life? Has there been a factor regarding manipulative behaviour, or co-dependent behaviour? The lessons we all need to learn are forgiveness, lack of judgement and unconditional love.

What relationships have you healed? Do be aware that when you send out healing on the spiritual plane to someone else, they will unconsciously become aware of the change in your relationship. Sometimes this can mean that the very person you wish never to see again pops into your life 'unexpectedly'. Just remember this meeting will have been synchronised by your angels in order for you to re-act in a different way at this coming together. The other person might still be the same, but bear in mind that you have changed, and therefore all the circumstances and beliefs around you have also changed. You can, of course, decide to revert to the old way of relating to this person, as though no healing took place, that is up to you. As time goes by you will be amazed at the change in yourself by doing these exercises.

WORKPAGE 5

Healing My Senses: Date:

Colour of my flower: Meaning:

....

Healing Relationships Date:

1. Person's name (optional)

Flower Meaning/Lesson

....

2. Person's name (optional)

Flower Meaning/Lesson

....

3. Person's name (optional)

Flower Meaning/Lesson

....

Now that you have gone through Exercise 8, keep the knowledge that you have done your part in the forgiveness process uppermost in your mind. Often we have been holding onto negativity for so long that we forget to let it go after doing a healing on it, because we've got into the habit of feeling certain emotions. It's these negative ties which are blocking our way forward, which are keeping our backs bent, our eyes focused down on the ground instead of looking upwards to heaven. If you accept you're tied to some people in order to learn certain lessons, then once you've done your part in healing your lesson you are free. However, the other party might not be on a 'learning curve' right now, and so there is still a tie between you. You, yourself, can cut the ties from your end in order to cancel the bond, but it is necessary to have the right intention should you do this. There are no short cuts. There is a lesson to be learned and only when it has will you be free to move on. If you try to cut the ties before you learn the lesson you will only find yourself tied to someone else, repeating the test again. Therefore, before undertaking the following exercise, be sure to have included the person involved in the 'Flowers of Forgiveness' visualisation, Exercise 8.

Exercise 9: Cutting the Ties

Ask your angel to be with you when you do this exercise. Find some time and space to yourself, without interruptions. Now go deep within, close your eyes and imagine yourself surrounded by blue light. Think of the person to whom you feel tied and, keeping yourself separate, surround this other person with blue light. Now imagine there is a tie of some kind keeping you both attached to each other. It can be of any material you visualise, such as a chain, a rope, a ribbon. Try now to either change its colour to blue or to surround it with blue light. Know that your angel is here beside you, holding a golden scissors in its hand. Know that you have done your part in the healing of this relationship. Now ask your angel to gently and lovingly cut the tie that binds you. Imagine your angel holding the golden scissors and now snipping the tie with gentleness and with love. Send love and light to the other person as you feel yourself cut free and moving slowly away from the scene. Thank your angel for being here today.

After doing this exercise you may find that the other party involved suddenly appears in your life again. It might be a phone call, a 'chance' meeting, a letter. Take any sudden connection as being the other's unconscious realising that the tie is now cut. Bless the person in your mind and know that you do not have to connect with them again. This is the last time you need be in contact. It is interesting to note how someone who was once of utmost importance in your life can apparently suddenly disappear from it, and you probably have hardly noticed! This is yet another example of you 'having learned the lesson'. Congratulations, you've passed the test!

There is a lot of talk about 'relationships'. Nowadays it tends to refer to only a sexual liaison, but the real meaning of the word is about relating to other people and things in your life. We have relationships with our mother and father, our sisters and brothers, our work colleagues, our neighbours, our pets, our career, food, perhaps alcohol and drugs, with money.... yes, it's all about how we relate to these people and things. The 'ship' is the journey of discovery we go on as we learn to have 'right relations' with those people and things that share our life. When we don't have right relations with money, for instance, we tend to hit rock bottom on the financial scale, when we don't have right relations with chemical substances we can become dependent on them, when we don't have right relations with ourselves, we have co- dependent relations with others. The list goes on.......... And the entire subject of 'relationships' is a learning process based on how we relate to ourselves.

Until we learn to relate to ourselves in a positive, caring, loving and non-judgemental way, we cannot have right relations with others. Everything we do, everyone we meet, every experience in our life is a reflection of how we relate to ourselves. Ask yourself now, how do I relate to myself? Do I see myself through other people's eyes? Do I judge myself by my looks, my weight, my figure, my career, my car, my home? Do I judge myself by my partner's career, car, income.....? Do I act as though I deserve to be treated with respect? Do I truly understand that I can only do my best, and I can never, ever do better than my best? Do I forgive myself for not being perfect? Do I show compassion to myself? It's up to you to go through those questions and answer them honestly. If you realise you've been hard on yourself, it's up to you to change your attitude. Then you will see how other people will relate to you in this positive,

supportive way. Remember, everyone in your life is simply a reflection of how you are relating to yourself.

Exercise 10: The Mirror Treatment

This is a very simple exercise you can carry out which will tell you in seconds exactly how you relate to yourself. Hold a mirror in your hand. Look deeply into your eyes, then *say your name aloud* and

'....I love you'.

Watch your reaction, feel your reaction. Was it easy to say 'I love you?' Did you feel like crying, did you turn away, did you feel a lump forming in your throat? If so, why? Why can't you love yourself?

Now take the mirror in your hand again. Look deeply into your eyes and *say your name aloud* and

'...... I forgive you for not being as I wanted you to be.
I forgive you and I set you free.'

How did you feel saying this? Was it difficult to forgive yourself? Say this as often as you feel is necessary. When a few days

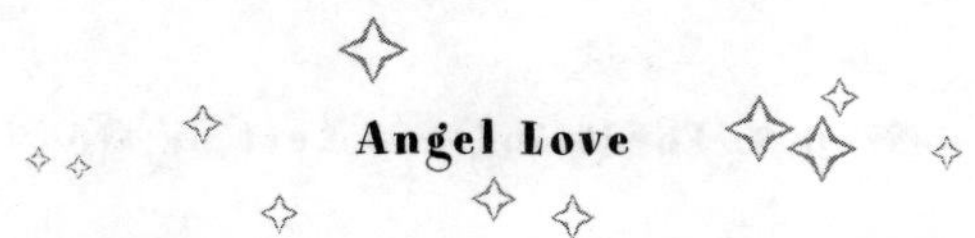

or perhaps a week has passed, try the 'I love you' treatment again. How does it feel now?

Be sure to keep a record of your 'Mirror Treatment' reactions on Workpage 6 (p. 133). See how you accept and love yourself the more you learn to forgive yourself for not being perfect. See how you reflect outwards your new self-image. You'll discover your circle of friends changes. There'll be no need now to have critical, unsupportive people in your life. Your new friends will prove to be loving and supportive because that's the reflection of the energy you will be sending out.

WORKPAGE 6

The Mirror Treatment

Attempt 1: Date:

My reaction

....

....

Attempt 2: Date:

My reaction

....

....

Attempt 3: Date:

My reaction

....

....

Attempt 4: Date:

My reaction

....

....

Step 4

Making the Breakthrough

'Beloved, let us love one another, because Love is from God.'

What is love? Love is energy. It's full of life and lightness, it brings feelings of joy and contentment to those who share it. It is not co-dependent, or conditional on someone acting in a certain way, or loving us back, even. Once upon a time, and this is not so long ago, I believed that love meant submission, or certain loss. In my mind I believed that if I gave my love to someone it would never be given back to me, I'd have lost it forever.

But I was wrong, I was looking at it the wrong way around. For when I offer love to someone I actually gain from the gift. I end up with more love than I offered in the first place. Now that's a miracle in itself! I discovered when love is flowing our lives are full of good things. Work situations prosper. Where once personality types challenged one another with the Love of Power they now co-mingle and co-operate. Instead of the Love of Power we can begin to see the Power of Love prospering. We begin to be offered gifts from others, perhaps just little things to begin with. So be aware of new avenues of sharing being opened up in your life. They might be miniscule to begin with, you might almost miss out on them, in fact. So let me offer some advice: whatever is offered to you, make a habit of accepting it, whether it's an unexpected cup of tea, a bunch of flowers, or a cheque for £50! Even if you don't want it, accept the gift and pass it on to someone else if you don't like it. By accepting 'your good' you are then opening up to accepting love in all areas of your life, for all time. I used to say 'No thanks, I can manage', and then wonder why I felt unloved! Now I say 'Thank you' and 'Thank you, angels!' whenever I'm offered any gift at all. It could be a parking space, it could be an offer of a holiday home for a short break. Try not to question it, accept it instead. Now I've opened up to accepting 'my good' it's coming to me all the time. Before this, there was a big 'CLOSED' sign on my door. And I wondered why I had no love in my life! If you've felt a lack of love in your life it might be difficult to accept unconditional love from someone else to begin with, but do try to be open and you'll be amazed at how your life begins to turn around.

True love is unconditional love, like the love you can enjoy from your angel. It has no rules. It is unconditional. There is no price to pay for it. Have you ever been offered something simply out of someone's generosity of heart? Have you thought twice about accepting it? I've done the same. Because of my 'history' I wondered 'What's the story behind this?' before daring to accept a gift. Remember the saying 'There's no such thing as a free lunch'? Well the good news is, there is! But to truly understand this and accept a free gift which comes from love, we must first learn to love ourselves, and that often requires us to forgive ourselves for our past actions. In that way we can begin to forgive others for their actions, and this is how unconditional love develops. When you practise unconditional love there is no need for anger, resentment, jealousy, prejudice, or any other negative emotions which find their source in fear. When we practise unconditional love we must receive unconditional love from others, because what we give out will always come back to us. And then, of course, we are getting even closer to our angels.

Love brings light into our lives and banishes the darkness. When you know that you are loved by your angel, completely and unconditionally, you will be able to say 'goodbye' to fear for ever. It's terribly sad how so often we live our lives surrounded by fear. Fear is the opposite of love. It's as simple as that. Fear is born out of lack of knowledge of God's love for us. Fear can only exist where there is darkness. Once the light of God's love, through our angels, comes into our lives, we cannot live in darkness, it's just impossible. Sometimes I meet people who are so fearful of death they forget to live. Then I remember 'Whoever does not know love does not know God, for God is love'. When you know that you are loved by your angel, a messenger sent to you personally by God, you can free your life from fear forever.

One of the big set-backs that we tend to face when opening up to our angel is fear. 'What if...?' questions such as 'What if my angel judges me?' tend to come into our mind the moment we sit quietly and try to open up to our angel. Your angel is there for you, loving and supportive, at all times. It doesn't matter about the past, that's history. It doesn't matter about the future, that's speculation. The only moment that matters is NOW. Angel time. The present. Angels know your good bits and your bad bits and they still love you. Well, if our angels loves us, regardless, isn't that a good starting point to love ourselves?

'Beloved, let us love one another, for Love is from God' is an important message for us to understand. It's a message from our angel. 'Let's get on together, we've been given this energy to share, it's from God, so why don't we go for it!' The message is clear: Love is from God. Love is a living energy which can quite literally bring us into harmony. Let's open up to our Angel's love because it's a gift from God.

Earlier I mentioned that 'Heaven' means 'Harmony' and 'Hell' means 'Wall' or 'Boundary'. It's those walls and boundaries that we need to dismantle in order to reach our Heaven on

Earth. All the lack of love in the world, in other words the war, the fighting, the bigotry, the prejudice, the apartheid, the neglect, is all based on walls forming boundaries around us which then make us feel fearful of the world outside. Often we watch pitched battles ensuing on our television screens and it seems impossible for us to actually make a difference, to do anything that might stop the bloodshed, the tears, the heartbreak. Were you around when Bob Geldof initiated 'Band Aid' and 'Live Aid'? It's some years ago now but I can still remember the great burst of hope I felt when I turned on the television and saw bands playing in the USA, the UK and the USSR, (then behind 'The Iron Curtain'), all working together with the one hope in mind, to help the people in Africa who had been devastated by famine. That original idea that Bob Geldof had, that we each could make a difference, took on its own energy and literally lit up the world!

Often it's very difficult for us sitting in our own homes to feel we could ever make a difference in the world-wide landscape. But just think for a moment, if each of us decided today to dismantle just one wall in our life, can you imagine the difference it would make? And when I say 'a wall' I mean something that is keeping our Love Energy from becoming one with someone else's Love Energy. I had a lovely experience some years ago when I gave a 'Talking With Angels' workshop in Derry in Northern Ireland. When we first met I never asked what religion, if any, the participants followed, it was of no interest to me. I was delighted to see that as the time went by any preconceived barriers simply and easily disappeared between the group members. They were each thrilled with the experiences they underwent during the workshop and offered a lot of support to one another during the time we spent together. I do often see angels manifesting in a group situation, but not always. When I was in Derry I 'inadvertently' put out an extra chair when was not required and then began the workshop. Half an hour into it I saw a Being of Light sitting on this 'empty' chair and moving its head gently as though listening intently to what I was saying. If ever I wondered if I was doing the right thing it was confirmed to me without a shadow of a doubt that weekend! The Angel stayed, the participants went out of their way to support each other, and I have very happy memories of the visit. As it happened, the venue turned out to be a special place set aside as a 'Centre for Peace and Reconciliation'. That weekend we each practised the suggestion 'Let us love one another because Love is from God' and there was no fear.

If we start off from a belief that we have chosen certain situations in this physical life in order to learn certain lessons on our journey of spiritual enlightenment, we must accept that we are responsible for what has happened to us in our life so far. If we chose our parents, that means that regardless of the amount of love they did or did not show us, we made the decision to come into that situation for some particular purpose. This does not exonerate either a father or mother from any abuse they may have heaped on their children. If this is the case, they are responsible for any abuse. But it does mean that we must ask ourselves, why did we chose this situation? Why did we chose to be ignored/ unloved/harshly treated/abused..........etc. What lessons were we to learn from it? Again, this does not condone any bad behaviour on any adult's part, it is merely a question we must ask ourselves: why did we chose this, what have we to learn from it? So often nowadays we hear of someone who perhaps sexually abused a child using the excuse 'I did it because I was abused as a child'. This is not acceptable. It is not the answer. If someone is abused as a child one lesson to be learned is not to abuse someone else, that is simply perpetuating the problem. So what could the lesson be? Perhaps it is 'heal yourself', move on, take responsibility for your own life rather than putting the blame on someone else. Then, and only then, can we say we have learned the lesson and shown unconditional love.

There are other hurts that happen to us as children. Perhaps our father or mother seemed, in our eyes, to reject us. As adults we can look back and think that maybe there could have been a reasonable explanation for it, i.e. our parents' marriage was going through a bad time, Mummy had a miscarriage, Daddy had lost his job, Granny had just passed on, money was tight.............. there is a myriad of possible reasons why our mother and father might not have been able to give us 100% attention 100% of the time. However, as a small child we are unable to reason this out because, until we reach 8 or 9 years of age, we are incapable of dealing with reason or logic. We just haven't learned it yet. Everything that happens to us tends at that time to be taken in on the emotional level. There is no logical, reasoning ability there for us to draw on. If Mummy goes into hospital to have another baby, the pre-logic child thinks 'Mummy's deserted me, I've been abandoned', while the older child who has learned logic reasons 'Mummy will be home soon and will be bringing a new baby'. Therefore there are totally different messages being understood about the same event depending on the age of the child!

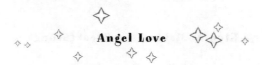

There is no doubt that what happens in our family is what becomes 'familiar' to us. Should a young woman live in a violent family situation it is almost assured that she will be drawn to someone who is violently abusive. It's not because she's stupid, it's just that this is what is 'familiar' to her. If someone comes from a safe, secure family where each member supports the other, this is the partner he or she will be drawn to. Again, it's what is 'familiar' to us. How often have you heard someone say of their spouse 'He/She's just like my father/mother!'

If we are shown an abundance of love as a child it is more than likely that we shall show an abundance of love as we go out

into the world. If we are shown that it is unsafe to love, that is what we shall show: love equals danger. It begins to manifest in us in our school days, in our work situation, in our social engagements and, of course, when we try to reach out to our angel. But if this is the case, it just means we've got the wrong message for it should say Love equals safety, Love equals security.

Holding onto the wrong message can lead to dis-ease in our emotional energy. Dis-ease simply means a 'lack of ease'. When our emotional energy or body has been hurt we tend to feel so distressed and so full of pain we try to close it down. Often the outcome can be what we now call 'work-aholism', when we turn away from feelings and commit ourselves to living in our 'mental body', our intellectual or thinking side, rather than our feeling side. In this case, every time an emotional pain begins to surface, we immediately turn to work again, spending all our waking lives in our mental body, desperately trying to tire ourselves out so that our emotions won't have a chance to affect us. Another outcome of emotional dis-ease can be in addiction of another sort. It can be addiction to alcohol, to drugs, to food, or even to a pattern of behaviour. We may try to dull the pain we feel by sedating it with alcohol, food or drugs, but no matter how much we consume, the pain is still there. The body will send us messages, such as emotional pain, telling us to heal our emotions. The pain itself is the message to get moving, it should not become a fatal dis-ease.

Having unsatisfying or destructive relationships with others is another sign of emotional dis-ease. If you find yourself constantly repeating patterns in your relationships, whether it's violence, emotional blackmail, co-dependency, dis-loyalty, then it's a sign that your emotional body needs healing. We are, after all, meant to have wonderfully fulfilling relationships with everyone who comes into our lives. If this isn't the case with you, don't give up, just decide to change. Emotions are energy, and when we close down our emotional body not only do we stop being able to relate to others, we also tend to stop being able to move another energy through our lives, and that's financial energy. So if you are facing a financial crisis in your life, consider if it may be connected with your ability to relate and share with others. Perhaps you feel that you don't deserve happiness because of something you said or did. Once you balance your emotions by healing them you will also be able to balance your bank statements!

Often, as adults, we are following patterns of behaviour that became familiar to us as a child. At the time we learned certain beliefs some of them were possibly very helpful, such as 'Don't talk to strangers', 'Mummy knows best', 'Do what your big sister/brother tells you', 'Watch your step', etc. However, there comes a time as we begin to find our own uniqueness when we should look again at such messages and see if they are appropriate to our current life.

The same goes for what we saw happening in our own backgrounds. Perhaps Mum and Dad didn't talk to each other, and fumed silently instead. As you all sat around your family dinner table did Dad say to you 'Tell your mother I'll be late tonight' while she told you 'Ask your father to pass the salt'? How do you deal with differences of opinion in your present life? Was Dad out philandering while Mum cried quietly at home, believing she was nothing without him? How do you view your own relationships? Do you feel 'nothing' without a 'better half' no matter how good or bad that other half is in reality? How did your

family react to financial support, did they believe it was always there for them or that counting pennies was a virtue? Or did Dad leave the family home and did Mum tell you 'You can't trust men, they're all the same!' If this is the case, can you now trust members of the opposite sex?

If such situations happened in your past, do bear in mind that we each chose our parents and our environments in order to learn lessons, so painful though it may seem, there is absolutely no point in passing the blame on to someone else. The important thing is to learn from the experiences, then we don't have to repeat them. As the saying goes 'Those who do not learn from history are destined to repeat it.'

It helps to imagine what would have been going on in your mother and father's time. They were children too, and had to go through those early years when they had no ability to assuage their hurts and pains through the use of logic, for all they had were their emotions, just like us. Spend a moment or two thinking about your parents' history. Were they brought up in an age of austerity during the Second World War? Did they have loving parents or was it a case of 'Children should be seen and not

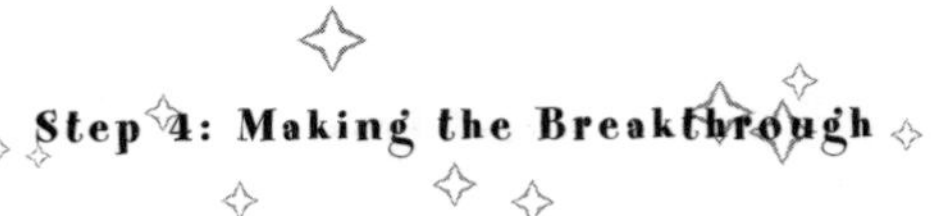

heard' or 'I'm staying because there's nowhere else to go'? Have you any idea how their siblings related to them? Do they speak to or about their sisters and brothers? There is a myriad of questions you can ask yourself about your parents' background, and their parents' background....all down the past generations. Have you ever seen photographs of them as children? Have you heard them talking about their history? Do they speak easily about their own childhood?

It's easy to see how we pick up beliefs from our family background and how we can allow these beliefs to become patterns of behaviour which, in the long run, bring us back again and again to the same self-defeating situation. It's like always trying to get out onto the main highway of life, and just when you think you've made it you discover it's another cul-de-sac. But the question is, how did you end up here yet again? If you want to answer that question, try the following exercise.

Exercise 11: Breaking the Pattern

Think of some area of your life where you feel you can never quite make it. It might be in love, in your career, in your self-

esteem, in your family relationships. Use the Workpages following to write out your history in this area. For instance, take a career problem. Write down your first job, why you took it and why you left. Then write down your second job, why you took it, why you left. If you're honest with yourself you will soon discover a pattern emerging in the chosen area of your life. Now that you have found that there is a pattern you can decide if you want to break it or not.

In my own case I spent several years having many a 'growth opportunity' in my financial status and my career. When I did this short exercise regarding my career I discovered that I hadn't ever actually had one! I'd had jobs, plenty of jobs, but never an actual planned career. The need for money had always kept me moving from place to place, from job to job. I had never given myself enough time to sit down and plan what I actually wanted in my life. Not once had I ever focused on my future in this way. I discovered that my life in this regard was really 'crisis management' rather than a focused and planned career. Once I found this out I could, of course, do something to change it. But until I made the discovery I was literally working in the dark!

WORKPAGE 7

BREAKING THE PATTERN OF MY CAREER

The history of my career:

....

....

....

....

....

....

....

....

....

....

WORKPAGE 8

BREAKING THE PATTERN OF MY ROMANTIC RELATIONSHIPS

The history of my romantic relationships:

....

....

....

....

....

....

....

....

....

....

WORKPAGE 9

BREAKING THE PATTERN OF MY BELIEF IN LIMITATIONS

The history of my abundance:

....

....

....

....

....

....

....

....

....

....

WORKPAGE 10

BREAKING THE PATTERN OF MY LACK OF SELF-EXPRESSION

The history of my ability to express myself openly:

....

....

....

....

....

....

....

....

....

....

WORKPAGE 11

BREAKING THE PATTERN OF MY EMOTIONAL BLOCKS

The history of showing my emotions:

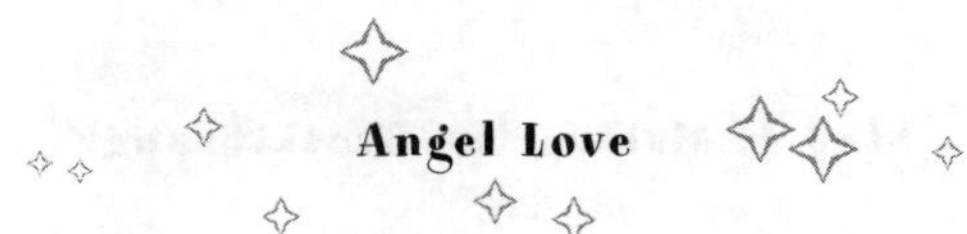

Exercise 12: Healing Parental Relationships

The following Visualisation exercise will help to heal the beliefs we might have brought with us from our childhood into our adult life. By healing the old, negative beliefs, we can be assured that we shall have the ability to enjoy healthy, loving relationships with our adult counterparts, without fear. If you do not know your parents you can still heal your relationship with them on the spiritual level.

As before, follow the steps in Exercise 2 regarding recording the visualisation, and remember to ground yourself first (Exercise 1). This is a suggested script and the visualisation should last 25 minutes approximately. Be sure to leave a lot of space between each instruction:

When you're in a comfortable position, take a deep breath and as you breathe in imagine there's a beautiful pink light travelling up your toes, across your feet and into your ankles, and as you breathe out allow any tension in this area to gently flow out into the ground below. And now your feet and ankles seem to gently turn into mist and disappear.

Now as you breathe in, the beautiful pink light travels up from your ankles into your calves, and moves up into your knees. And as you breathe out allow any tension here to gently flow out into the ground below. And now your calves and knees seem to gently turn into mist and disappear.

Now breathe in the pink light into your upper torso. See the pink light travel into your heart and into your lungs. Now it moves up into your shoulders. And as you breathe out allow any tension here to gently flow out into the ground below. And now your upper torso and your shoulders seem to gently turn into mist and disappear.

As you breathe in, the beautiful pink light travels all around your shoulders, releasing any knots and tension there. It flows gently down into your upper arms, your lower arms. It's flowing into your wrists, your hands and all the way down into your finger tips. Now as you breathe out any tension in these areas gently flows down into the ground below. And now this whole area of your body seems to gently turn into mist and disappear.

Now breathe in the beautiful pink light up into your throat and into your neck. The pink light releases any blocks in your throat and you find it easier to express yourself creatively. And now the pink light moves up into the back of your head, And as you breathe out any tension here gently flows out into the ground below and as it does so, it's as though this area of your body gently turns into mist and disappears.

Watch as the pink light moves up into your ears, then it moves into your chin and your mouth, into your nose, up into your eyes and your forehead. Now the pink light moves into your scalp and goes all the way up to the crown of your head. And as you breathe out any tension here gently flows into the ground below, while your head seems to gently turn into mist and disappear. And you are assured that the Earth will recycle anything you have given it and turn it into Light.

You know now that you are a being of pure pink light, the colour of love. How wonderful it is to be this healing pink light.

You are now feeling light and carefree and completely relaxed. And I want you to imagine that you're standing on the top of a hill. Look around you. See the beautiful valley below, and the mountaintops in the far distance. Enjoy the clear, fresh air as you breathe in and out, slowly and deeply. Listen to the sounds of the silence. Feel the light breeze gently move around you. Let the rays of the sun gently warm you. How peaceful it is here.

Look down at your feet and see a path before you. It is time to follow this pathway. As you move down, down, down from the hill, you notice the green fields around you and you hear birds singing in the clear air. You feel happy and relaxed. Then you hear a different sound. It's the sound of water gently tumbling down from the hill. As you come closer to the sound you realise that a waterfall is forming a pool, like a small lake. How inviting it seems. Watch as the sunlight plays on the surface of the sparkling clear water of the pool. As you listen you hear the gentle lap of the small waves at the water's edge as the tide comes in and out, in and out. Listen to the gentle sound. It's like the sound of the emotions, coming in and moving out. Coming in and moving out.

You decide to go into the water. It's so inviting. You know you are safe, for the pool is not very deep. You walk slowly into the water. It's much warmer than you had thought. Yet it's refresh-

ing as well. How wonderful it feels to have the water touch your body. It's as though you are weightless. Just drifting and floating. Floating and drifting. Completely safe. Completely secure.

And now you realise your angel is close by. Your angel is supporting you in everything you do. You lie back in the placid water and allow your body to float gently on the surface. Your angel is supporting you. It's a wonderful feeling of freedom as you look up into the clear blue sky and see birds circling high above.

Your angel wants to help you heal your relationship with your mother. Your angel helps you to see your mother as a baby. Just watch for a moment. See this little baby coming into the world, completely helpless. See your mother's reaction when she was first born. How much love did she receive? Were her cries heard? What were her hopes for her life? Was she cuddled and kissed? Did she get the love she needed from her mother? Did she get the love she needed from her father? Did she feel warm and comforted, or did she feel alone and fearful? Know that it is alright to cry now if you wish. Crying is simply releasing blocked up emotions. Crying frees these emotions.

What would you do if your mother was that baby now? Could

you lift her up into your arms and cuddle her? Could you comfort her? Could you give her all the love she needed so that she could pass on that love to you when you were a baby? If you find it difficult to show love to your mother, ask your angel and your mother's angel to come to you now and help you both heal any and all wounds that you are holding in your hearts.

(LEAVE A LONG PAUSE HERE)

And now your angel wants to help you heal your relationship with your father. Your angel helps you to see your father as a baby. Just watch for a moment. See this little baby coming into the world, completely helpless. See your father's reaction when he was first born. How much love did he receive? Were his cries heard? Know that it is alright to cry now if you wish. Crying is simply releasing blocked up emotions. Crying frees these emotions.

What were his hopes for his life? Was he cuddled and kissed? Did he get the love he needed from his mother? Did he get the love he needed from his father? Did he feel warm and comforted, or did he feel alone and fearful? What would you do if your father was that baby now? Could you lift him up into your arms and cuddle him? Could you comfort him? Could you give him all the love he needed so that he could pass on that love to you when you were a baby? If you find it difficult to show love to your father, ask you angel and your father's angel to come to you now and help you both heal any and all wounds that you are holding in your hearts.

(LEAVE A LONG PAUSE HERE)

When you are ready, allow yourself to drift safely and gently on the water. As the water moves around your body you know now that your emotions are being healed. There is no need now to have them blocked and locked away any more. You can enjoy a great sense of relief as this knowledge washes over you. And now you find yourself on the shore again, with the sun gently warming your body and feeling a warm breeze touch your skin. You know that your emotions are healing and you feel a surge of joy move through your body.

Now you know you can share love again, and your angel wants to give you a gift to remind you of this healing. Look into your hands and see what you have been given. Remember you will always have this gift to help you show love.

And now you begin to walk up the path which leads you to the hill where you began your journey. You climb up, up, up the pathway. You are now on the small hill where you started out. And, taking a deep breath you now breathe out and once more you can feel the ground beneath you. And taking another deep breath in as you breathe out you can feel your fingers and toes. And now, taking a final deep breath in and out, you now return to this room, feeling relaxed, refreshed and much more loved than before.

If you found you are emotionally distressed during this visualisation, do allow yourself to unblock the stopper that's holding back your tears. Tears are Nature's way of freeing our emotions and washing ourselves clean of our past. Tears allow the hormone seratonin into our bloodstream, a hormone which is a natural relaxing agent. A good cry now and again really helps us start afresh, it's like the day after a tremendous thunder and lightning storm, when the air is fresh and clear again after a time of heavy oppression. So don't be afraid to let go!

WORKPAGE 12

Healing Parental Love

Record any emotion or insight you might have gained during the Visualisation.

Insights regarding my mother:

....

....

Insights regarding my father:

....

....

The gift I received to heal the relationship between myself and my parents:

....

....

Step 5:

Opening Your Heart to Angel Love

'Know Only That You are Loved'

I received the message 'Know only that you are loved' when I was going through one of my many 'growth' periods. It was very welcome, especially as it was such a time of transformation for me. Now that you have begun the process of healing relationships you will find that your life begins to be transformed in many ways, some of which are immensely satisfying, while others might make you feel unsettled and unsure. That fearful time before changing can

feel like hanging onto a cliff edge but not daring to let go. When you do allow yourself to jump free from the past you will be surprised how much easier life can become, but the initial moments before change can seem terrifying. It's probably the same before the chrysalis becomes the butterfly, before the snake's old skin has completely sloughed off to allow the new to grow. Yet these changes are essential for natural growth. Have you seen those fantastic designs made of dominoes when just one domino has to be touched and the entire picture is transformed? That one tiny change ensures that there is a continuing change in the entire domino design and this is what happens in our lives when we transform even a tiny aspect of our way of living.

Now that you've begun to change you will find that the people in your circle, those who were reflections of your old self, will either begin to change themselves or else move out of your life. At this crucial time you may be accused of 'changing', as though that were a bad thing, or of being crazy, or of joining a 'cult', or of 'letting us down', etc. Try to understand that those who say such things are merely clinging onto the cliff edge themselves, terrified to see you changing because they unconsciously know they are being challenged to move on themselves. Change is often difficult: it can manifest in the loss of support from erstwhile friends, finances and family as you are no longer willing to continue what is possibly showing up as a charade to you. Inside you know that change is essential for growth so it must happen. Ask your angels for extra help at this difficult time and keep a record of your dreams, those nightly messages which are offering you a new blueprint for your life.

One of the Angel Cards I mentioned earlier has a picture of an angel carrying a white flag and under this is the word 'Surrender'. This is what we must do when we open up to our angels. 'Surrender' does not mean 'submission', it simply requires us to surrender our ego or conscious self, and open up to our true spirituality. You may immediately think you are losing control if you surrender, a natural response when you consider our ego is only 10% of our being, while our spirit is 90%, for the ego immediately fears being over-whelmed. But once we surrender to the fact that our angels know what is best for us – and they must for they have come to us from God – then

we will find ourselves placed firmly on that path of enlightenment and facing in the right direction as well! Surrendering will allow that 90% of our essence, our spirit, to lead us onwards, instead of submitting to the possibly flawed directions of our ego, flawed because it is fearful. By surrendering, we shall be connected to that great 'Internet' of spiritual knowledge and unconditional love. And knowledge is power, self-power.

If you have followed the earlier steps of this book, you will be well on the way to healing your body, your mind, your emotions and your spirit. These four areas of our life work together 'holistically', each part affecting the other either positively or adversely. If you were emotionally blocked you will find that now you are healing this area of your life other aspects will change too. Excess weight, especially around the second chakra, (the stomach area), is often a sign of emotional blockage, and when you are looking after this area of your life you will find that this excess which has acted as a 'buffer' between you and others will probably begin to dissipate simply because it is no longer needed. Money, which is simply another form of energy based on notions of self-worth, will also begin to flow when the emotions are healed. Other signs of healing and renewal will be seen in positive 'self-fulfilling prophecies' in your life, that is good things coming about because that is what you are prophesying with positive thought forms and the aid of your angels. With regular relaxation and guided imagery exercises your physical energy will be renewed and revitalised, and being in touch with your angels will enlighten your spirit.

Exercise 13: Recording your Path of Transformation

Think back to when you first opened this book. If you have been following the suggested exercises and visualisations, ask yourself how has your life changed? Using Workpage 13 (p. 171), list any areas of your life which are beginning to transform, such as relationships with your partner, parents, siblings, friends, colleagues, yourself and, of course, your angels!

Record any changes in your career, your finances, your home. You might prefer to record a percentage change e.g.:

'relating to sister, 10% improvement,' with today's date. Then update the list as each week or month goes by. By the way, often when we begin the process of transformation life can seem to become worse. Don't despair if this is the case! It's similar to having wounded a limb and putting a plaster over it in order to heal. There comes a time when that plaster has to be taken off so that the complete healing can take place and you can show your newly-healed limb to the world. But sometimes the act of pulling off that plaster really hurts! Yet it lasts for such a short time, and the end result is a limb with new skin, fully healed. Pain at this crucial time is a wonderful message saying you are on the path of transformation. Look forward, not backward. Constantly ask your angel to show you the way and support you. Remember, you are never alone but you must ask for help.

WORKPAGE 13

TRANSFORMATION LIST

Relationship	% Improvement	Date
....	....	....
....	....	....
....	....	....
....	....	....
....	....	....
....	....	....
....	....	....
....	....	....
....	....	....
....	....	....

Once you have decided to surrender to your angels you know that you can not only have anything you wish for in life, but you can have *everything*: a good home, a wonderful relationship, a happy and fulfilling work atmosphere which satisfies you in every way. Unfortunately some of us have been brought up to believe that if someone is rich then that wealth must have come about by immoral means, and so we tell ourselves that money corrupts, it's 'ill gotten gains'. Yes, some people have made their riches through taking from others, but it is those people who have been corrupt, not the money! There is more than enough for need, but there will never be enough for greed. Money is just money.

We sometimes believe that if we enjoy today something awful might happen tomorrow... well, those negative beliefs should have left you now that you have surrendered to your angels. Know only that you are loved, and therefore all that you wish for can be yours, for when you know you are loved you will always act with the right intention.

You can ask your angel to help your wishes come true, by making out a simple 'Wish List'. Do be aware they will come true, so be absolutely certain that what you wish for is what you do actually want. Be as specific as possible. For instance, if you put down on your Wish List that you want a man, you will get a man, but he may be an alcoholic, a sociopath..... do I need to go on? So, state the type of man you wish for: a loving, supportive, generous, healthy man, for instance. Or if you are unsure what to specify, put 'The perfect man for me right now'. The same would work for a job. You could be offered a job, one that doesn't pay, that proves to be exhausting, where you are surrounded by unsupportive people..... So state 'The perfect job for me right now' or 'A job which can become my career, fulfilling emotionally, financially and intellectually, with wonderfully supportive workmates....' And remember, it will come about for you in Angel Time, which is the right time for you.

Exercise 14: Making a Wish List

Use Workpage 14 (p. 174) to make out your Wish List. It's a simple step by step process: Step 1: Make your wish. Step 2: Surrender it to your angels. Step 3: Step back, and don't interfere. You've made your request, it's on it's way to you. Yes, life really is simple, especially when you have a little angelic help!

WORKPAGE 14

MY WISH LIST

My wish is: Date:

....

....

....

....

....

....

....

....

....

....

This last visualisation will help to heal your heart and begin afresh in your ability to love, regardless of any past 'history' you have been carrying in your life. By healing the four areas of your life you can now be more open to accepting all the love that is there for you from your angel.

Exercise 15: Open Your Heart to Angel Love

Find a quiet place to be and ensure that you will not be disturbed for a full 30 minutes. By now you understand the importance of regular, deep breathing in order to help you let go of any tension and relax into a visualisation exercise. Take your time recording the following script, it should run from 25-30 minutes. If you wish, play music softly in the background as you speak. Remember you can change the word 'you' to 'I' if you wish.

When you are comfortable begin to breathe in slowly and rhythmically. Listen to your inward and outward breath. Go down to your feet and imagine those tiny roots are growing from the soles of your feet into the ground below. Now imagine

you are breathing into every cell of your body. Feel the pores of your skin gently open to increase the depth of your breathing. You are now able to feel yourself breathing directly into your central core. The deeper the breath, the more relaxed you become. It's lovely and peaceful, and you know that your body is benefiting from this exercise. How easy it is becoming to relax and visualise. You welcome these moments. It is becoming second-nature to you.

As you go deeper and deeper within yourself you begin to remember the past. Go back in years and remember all the people you have loved. Remember the pain in your heart when you found they no longer loved you. What did it feel like? Did it leave a dark space in your heart? Are there scars there now, scars left from the hurt? Are they like huge holes or fissures? Are they small cracks which are difficult to close? What do you need to heal these scars? Invite your angel into your heart. Your angel brings you whatever you need. It helps to heal the scars. Now the scars are being healed. The darkness is leaving your heart. Your heart is no longer heavy, the burden of pain is leaving your heart.

Rest for a while as your heart is being healed. Now remember the joy of being loved and of loving. Remember how your heart lifted when you shared time with someone you cared for and who cared for you. Remember the wonderful feeling when you shared love from your heart with someone else.

Now I want you to imagine that your angel is in front of you. You may feel it, you may see it, or you may just sense it. You know your angel wants to share its love with you, it doesn't want you to feel separated or isolated anymore. Feel yourself holding out your arms to your angel. You feel no fear, you feel only love. Allow your tears to flow if this is right for you, for they will become tears of joy.

Now sense your angel is hugging you. You know with absolute certainty that your heart is now open to angel love. See a ray of golden light coming from your angel's heart into your own. It's as though a door opens in your heart to receive this love. Each time you breathe in, the golden light of your angel's love enters your heart, and each time you breathe out, any fear or tension leaves it. And as you breathe in again, your heart is once more filled with love, and as you breathe out any tension

or negativity leaves it. And as you breathe in, your angel's love heals any scars of hurt or pain in your heart, and as you breathe out, you release any pain, now and forever. And as you breathe in, your angel's love lights up any dark areas in your heart and as you breathe out, you release any darkness now and forever.

You continue to breathe in your angel's love until it feels as though your heart is completely filled with love. And now you know you have so much love you can actually share it with your angel. So now, as you breathe out an arc of golden light moves out from your heart and into your angel's heart. And as you breathe in your angel's love, you breathe out love to your angel. And now you see there's a circle of love moving between you and your angel. How wonderfully full of love you feel. And you know that you will never forget this moment. You have never felt such lightness, such joy or such love.

You realise there is so much love here that you would like to share it. You feel light and carefree, completely buoyed up by the lightness of your angel's love. You know you can leave this place now, quite safely, and fly with your angel to any place in your world which needs love right now. It's easy. Allow yourself to lift off the ground gently and fly with your angel. Your angel is helping you, supporting you. You know you are safe. You know you are loved. Now that you've left all the weight of negative living behind you are free and light and filled with love.

Now you want to visit some place in your life which feels a lack of love. Perhaps it's your home, your family, your place of work. You can go to all these places. It's easy, it's right, it's being visited with angel love. You see these places as being colourless, as being grey because there's no love there. But now as you fly over these places with your angel you see a great change taking place. It's as though it's raining love. The energy of angel love is lighting up these places and the people who are there. Look down and see what happens when the light reaches them. Invite those people out of their greyness, into the light of love. Call to them to come and meet their own angel. See their reaction! Do their faces change? Do their faces light up with love? See how the entire environment changes when it's touched by angel love. The light of angel love has transformed the negativity into joy. Watch the effect!

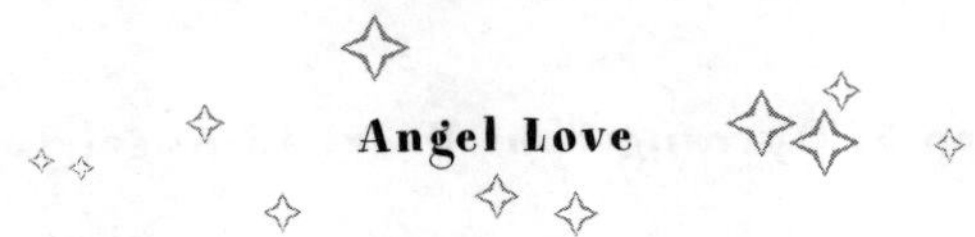

Now it's time to leave and return to where you began this journey. But know that you can come back here whenever you wish, to enjoy sharing love between yourself and your angel.

And now I want you to take a deep breath and as you breathe in and out once more you can feel the ground beneath your feet. And now as you breathe in and out again, you can now feel your fingers and toes. And now as you breathe in and out it's time to open your eyes, and you do so, coming back into this room, feeling relaxed, refreshed and much better than before.

Now that you have opened your heart to angel love remember how simple and natural it is to share your life with you angel. The love is there for us all, so let's share it.

Some Genuine Responses:

From Anya, Belgium:

'I attended your angel workshop in Mortsel, Belgium, on Saturday (28th February) and there is now something I would like to share with you. In the first visualisation, that was all about meeting your angel, and receiving a gift I saw a man, named Daniel, give me a star that had a blueish light shining from the inside. I remember I wasn't really sure at first about the shape, at first I thought it was a ball, and yet it was also a star, it was both...

'Now, as it happens, I went to do some shopping this evening after work. I also paid a visit to the shop that was next to the shop I first

went, just to stroll, I did not intend to buy anything in particular. I happened to pass a bunch of articles that were now down in price "all for 1 Euro" it said... and I started to look at everything. Suddenly I noticed an object, it was a toy thing, a kind of star shaped object in several colours available and if you push it, it has lights glowing on the inside (flickering, like a disco ball). It was available in pink, in lilac and in blue...

'All of a sudden I had to think about the visualisation I had in which Daniel gave me a star shaped ball (it was both star and ball) with a blue light glowing on the inside... I could hardly believe it, but here it was. It is an ugly thing actually, the object is made of some kind of rubber, but it is a ball with star shapes around it, it is blue and there are lights on the inside... Of course I bought it.

'I remembered during the workshop you said when your angel is trying to contact you, it will be in a way that only you will understand. I truly believe that this is a sign from my angel. It must be. It is too much of a coincidence.'

From Pauline, England.

'Here is my proof that Angels do exist: feeling in despair one day over my husband's ill-health, I lit a candle & asked for a sign that my Angel was with me. Here's a photo of what happened, I was amazed to see that the melting wax had built up at the back of the candle to form an Angel, I have burnt numerous candles before & since but this is the first time this has happened. I feel truly blessed & call it 'my candle of hope'. I got someone to take a photo & scan it back to my PC, so I could share it with others....,' The photo Pauline sent me clearly shows the silhouette of a beautiful pink angel made from the wax of the burning candle. It shows the head and wings on either side. A remarkable sight!

From Annemie, Belgium:

As a child, my mother taught me to speak with deceased relatives when I had problems, and I have a diary which is a conversation with my father and the angels (they surprise me sometimes with their answers!) Since opening up to angels more in recent years, the major change is that I feel more confident than before as I realise that there are energies beyond the visible and I can express myself

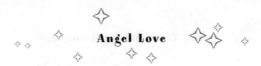

about this. Before meeting you (by reading the book which was the first step) I felt alone with it, and it is important to know that there are a lot of people who have this belief, who want the best for all, who want to learn to love oneself and others, who want to take care of the planet, who are against war, betrayal etc..

Also I experience that everything is coming at the right moment, in the right place, with the right people... and as this happens more and more, my faith is growing and...........fear is leaving! And that is for me the most important thing! Fear leaves ... love comes in !!!

FROM JENNIE, ENGLAND:

Having read 'Angel Magic' and loved it, I knew I had to contact you, but kept ignoring the little voice until one day I did. I think it was about April 2002 and to phone you I had to overcome many fears, mainly I had never phoned an author to tell them how much I liked their book before, you were adorable and I don't know if you remember but I cried down the phone!!! At that time I was just getting used to communicating with my Angels and felt cold and cried a lot, you were very kind and reassuring. Since then I have done loads of clutter clearing from my home, soul and heart and you helped me

see the way. The next stage was asking you to come and do a workshop at my house which was also a big step and how fabulous were both events we had here. Everyone that came enjoyed the days, they were fun, laid back, chatty and inspiring.

Since opening up to your books and attending your workshop, you (and the angels) have helped me get on the right path and discover that I can be real within this work. The daily effort I thought necessary was not so and your books helped me achieve a balance and forgiveness for past life traumas and achievements. You came to me at a time when I was not acknowledging my inner needs and intuition – life had taken over and a re-direction was needed. Angels had already made themselves apparent to me but I hadn't realised that messages they had were for me.

Caroline Brown Bishopbriggs Glasgow.

Since reading angel magic, I have become familiar and comfortable with my angels. I have also found Margaret to be one of the most down to earth and inspiring women I know. Go on, open your heart!

Angel Love

Nathalie, Netherlands:

I have been reading a lot of books that I could find about the angels and I bought angelcards and I learned so much about them! I know now that my grandmother is watching over me and that everything is going to be alright.. I learned also that it is not difficult to contact them, if you are ready to be still and listen. I also wanted to help other people with the cards, to help them to understand what the angels want to give with all there love and care. It gives me a very happy feeling when I know nothing about a person, and then to give helpful messages through the angels that they need at that moment. It is not my doing, I know, it's because the angels are helping. I hope you come to Holland soon! Since the first day that I started to read your book Angel Magic my life has changed very much and little wonders have come my way. Now I want to share it with people around me and help them when they are needing it. The strangest thing is that people listen to me and they are very pleased and looking at me with much belief. I know that's the work off the angels...!

Elaine, Carnuath, Scotland

I bought your book before going on holiday to Cyprus. I have a fear of flying and I opened your book after take off and as I read through the pages an incredible sense of calm came over me. On the way home I felt relaxed and kept talking to my newly-found angel. What a difference!

From Amanda, Middlesex, England

I just wanted to let you know that I found your books at a time in my life when I truly needed a friend. I rediscovered angels and that child like awe and belief in them and haven't looked back! That was just about three years ago and each and every day I count my blessings and chat with my angels at length about everything.

Before I start the day I spend ten minutes in my garden sitting on a bench under the trees and speak to my Guardian Angel. Sometimes I just open up and that's when I feel him around me wrapped up in his wings (usually his wings tickle the side of my face). I hope you don't think I'm totally mad but since reconnecting with angels I have been developing my psychic abilities at the College for Psychic Studies and I always call upon the angels for help. It's amazing what happens, the signs you get from them: from feathers on the ground in front of you, birds song when you least expect to see or hear a bird, or the most profound when a close friend tells you the answer conversationally on the same day you have asked for help. In lots of ways if I had not had a crisis that made me stop and evaluate my life and its purpose I would probably be another statistic on anti depressants. I always feel looking back that the escalation of my son's hyperactivity and exclusion from school was the only way to get me to stop look and listen to the spirit and angels around me. At college I always used to say that I needed a real 'road to Damascus' revelation to get going . Fortunately I'm not such a drama queen now and when I feel vulnerable or low I just smile to myself and call upon my angels for solace and comfort and I can truly say I have never been disappointed.

FROM MAI, JAPAN:

I want to share an experience I once had a couple of years ago. I am not sure if it was an angel experience or not. At that time, I thought it might have been a "kind ghost" or spirit. It was in the morning, around spring time and the sun shone so bright and beautiful. It was quite peaceful outside in contrast to what was going on in my mind and soul. I was still lying in my bed unable to get up. Just lying and crying and crying and crying. (The reason for my crying is not so relevant here). It was one of these time where I felt most unloved and alone and everything looked so dark and black – no present no future no nothing......... I was just feeling sorry for myself, so I just let all the tears out. I remembered I reached out my hand, because I just wanted so desperately to hold someone else's hand. I close my eyes and after a while I could feel another hand holding my hand. It was the most warmest and loving hand I have ever held. I was scared to open my eyes so I just kept them closed. Another thing, which I found very strange, was that while I was holding "someone else's" hand, I could hear footsteps right beside my bed. Many, many footsteps as if there were a lot of people walking from my bedroom to the balcony.(The footsteps were quite loud) I wasn't afraid, actually I got more and more calm. I felt very peaceful and the sound of the footstep continued for a couple of minutes. Then it disappeared and I was still lying in bed with closed eyes. I stopped crying and after a while I felt asleep again.

Well, I am not sure what this experience was. It might not have anything to do with angels. Maybe I was in an emotional distress

and "imagined" all this. But the "hand" and the sound of the footsteps were just as real to me as my tears. Before ever reading about angels or having any interest in them, I always wondered why I could sense some kind of "love", "kindness", "everything will be all right- feeling" whenever I found myself in my darkest hours. I somehow knew or felt I was been helped and supported but I just couldn't figure out why or what "it" was. No matter how dark the situation could get, I felt an "invisible" hand helping me emotionally. Now, I am very happy to find out that angels do exist and are always sending their messages of love to all of us. So, now from time to time I light a candle or burn an incense to thank the angels.

From Corinne, England:

It's the little things that make a difference. I feel the angels guiding me in many ways. Whereas life was always a battle, particularly in business, they guide me to meet the right people, see the right things, make the right decisions. Not only has my life changed for the better, they're having a positive effect in those around me, too. I have so much co-operation and love in both my work and home. Thank you, angels!

From Akemi, Japan:

Your book moved me to tears. Of course I tried to talk to my Angel and I made an "Angel Magic Circle", I had lots of fun! I can't hear Angel's voice yet, but I can feel them! I had many mystic experiences lately. I know my guardian angels. You wrote about angels, and many people felt happy. I'm so happy everyday, because I'm with my guardian angels, and I know they love me ! Sometimes I can get some messages from my angels, Archangels and The Virgin Mary. I can't thank you enough for you and your book "Angle Magic", it is my treasure.

If you have enjoyed this book you may wish to know that the following books are by Margaret Neylon:

'Angel Magic' (Thorsons, 2001)

'An Angel a Day' (Element, 2003)

The following products are also available :

Guided visualisations on audio-cassette and CDs with Margaret Neylon as follows:

'Angel Love'

'Angel Magic'

Angel Inspiration Cards (boxed set of 50 'angelic messages')

Margaret Neylon gives workshops and can be contacted at

Angelgate
Virginia, Co Cavan, Ireland
http://www.margaretneylon.com
angelgate@eircom.net